CREATING WEB PAGES

NICK VANDOME

In easy steps is an imprint of Computer Step
Southfield Road . Southam
Warwickshire CV47 0FB . United Kingdom
www.ineasysteps.com

Notice of Liability
Every effort has been made to ensure that this book contains accurate and current information. However, Computer Step and the author shall not be liable for any loss or damage suffered by readers as a result of any information contained herein.

Trademarks
All trademarks are acknowledged as belonging to their respective companies.

Printed and bound in the United Kingdom

ISBN 1-84078-280-3

Contents

Planning a site

Websites were once the preserve of the computer community or big business. However, with the rapid growth of the Internet and the World Wide Web it is now possible for anyone to create a website. Despite some appearances to the contrary this can be a painless and cheap experience and this chapter covers some of the basics for setting the groundwork before the Web authoring process begins.

Covers

Chapter One

Web page overview

An intranet is a network of computers in a closed environment such as an office. Intranets use the same technology as the Internet and information can be distributed via Web pages. This has the advantage that everyone who has access to the intranet can view information at the same time and it is also very flexible in relation to updating items.

There can have been few communication tools that have had such a rapid and far-reaching impact as the Internet. It embraces all areas of society, from business to entertainment, and from shopping to sport. It has reached the point where it has ceased to be a novelty and is now seen as an accepted part of everyday life. Because of this, it is becoming increasingly common for people to take an interest in creating their own pages and sites on the World Wide Web (WWW) or internal networks. This could be for social purposes, to promote themselves or a particular hobby; for business purposes for someone who runs their own business; or as a worker who is involved in creating and maintaining an office intranet. Before anyone begins creating their own Web pages, it is important to understand all of the elements that make up the Internet, with the World Wide Web being just one of them.

Elements of the Internet

If an attachment is included with an email the recipient has to have the appropriate program for opening the attachment. For instance, if a video clip is sent, the recipient will require a program such as RealPlayer or Windows Media Player. If in doubt, contact the person first, before the attachment is sent.

- Email. This is possibly one of the most important, and most widely used, elements of the Internet. It enables people to send electronic messages anywhere in the world in a matter of seconds. In addition, it is now possible to include a variety of attachments with an email, such as photographic images, video clips and sound files. Anything that can be converted into a digital format can be attached to an email. Email is sometimes referred to as a "killer app" (killer application) in terms of gaining widespread acceptance for the Internet

- World Wide Web. This is what some people think of as the Internet but it is in fact just one part of it. This is the collection of sites and pages that users view via a Web browser. There are millions of pages on the World Wide Web and this book is intended to show how you can create your own presence there

A Web browser is a piece of software that enables people to view Web pages. The most commonly used is Internet Explorer, followed by Netscape Navigator.

- Newsgroups. These are special interest groups to which users can contribute via emails that are sent (and viewed) to an area that is visible by all members of the group

- Chat rooms. These can be used to have real time audio or video conversations with other users

Elements of a Web page

The variety of designs of Web pages on the Internet is almost as diverse as the number of pages themselves. However, there are some basic elements that should be included in all Web pages:

It is essential that users feel confident about navigating around a website. If it is confusing, or they feel they may get lost within the site, they will quickly move on to somewhere else.

Navigation system. This enables the user to move to the main areas within the site

Other items that can be used to give Web pages extra functionality include:

- *Site search facility*
- *Page hit counter*
- *Date and time stamp*
- *News ticker*

A hyperlink (or link) is a piece of code written in HyperText Markup Language (HTML). HTML is a computer code that is used to create most pages on the Web. A hyperlink contains an instruction to the Web browser to take the user to the Web page specified in the link. A link is activated when it is clicked on by the user.

Hyperlinks. These allow users to "jump" to other pages, or email addresses, within the site or to other sites on the Web

Main content. This should be designed for presentation on-screen, rather than converted directly from hard copy content

Types of sites

Before you start creating your own Web pages and building them into a site it is worthwhile to look at the different types of sites that are on Web. These differ in design and style, according to their target audience.

Personal sites

These are sites that are created by individuals and contain information ranging from their favorite hobby to details about their pet snake.

Since the style and design of personal sites is entirely at the discretion of the individual concerned, the quality of them can be extremely variable. If you look at a lot of these sites, you may get more of an idea about what you do not want to include on your own pages, rather than what you do want to include.

The Personal Page of:

Nick Vandome

E-mail me!

Small business sites

These are sites that are intended to promote small and local business. They are frequently created by the people involved with local or small businesses. Small business sites should be clear, concise and give the user all of the details that they require.

Most small businesses should use the Web as a supplement to their real-world operations, not as the core part of it. This is not to say that a website cannot become a valuable part of a small business – but do not put all of your eggs in one Cyberspace basket.

DRCC

Corporate Communications

Writing and creative services

DRCC can help in the planning, structuring and production of print, electronic and face-to-face media.

The **media** we cover vary from advertisements to web sites - including brochures, case studies, feature articles, intranet material, newsletters, speeches and press conferences, to name only a few.

Our **key services** are -

- Research
- Writing
- Editing
- Proofreading
- Design
- Picture research
- Photography

About us

Strategic planning

Writing and creative services

Communication measurement

International communication

Training

Project and event management

What clients say about us

How to contact us

Large business sites

A lot of large businesses now have a presence on the Web. In most cases these are professionally designed sites that contain information about the company, its products and services and how to part with your money.

Large business sites are useful sources for design ideas and styles. Since a lot of them are designed by professional Web designers, they should display some of the latest design techniques.

Online business sites

These are sites that are run by businesses that only have an online presence. They tend to be e-tailers or multi-channel sites or cover topics such as entertainment or sport.

Matching format to audience

As with any form of publishing, it is important to know who your audience for your Web pages is going to be and to select a format accordingly. Some issues to consider in relation to this are:

- A young audience may require a more dynamic and visually striking format

- An older audience may require a more conservative style, that is clear and straightforward

- A business audience will want to be able to find the relevant information as quickly as possible

- If the site is being used to sell products, users will want to see as much product information as possible and also be assured that the online purchase process is as secure as it can be

- All users will want a navigation system that enables them to move around the site quickly and easily

As we get older our eyesight deteriorates. If you are creating a site for an older audience, bear this in mind and use a font of a reasonable size and clarity.

A conservative style for Web pages does not mean they have to be dull. If it is done well, this type of format will have a clean and classical feel to it.

Work out who is going to be the intended audience for your website, before you begin creating the pages.

The format of websites can vary dramatically, depending on the target audience

Creating guidelines

If you are creating pages for a commercial website (either an external website or an intranet) it is essential that you have guidelines from which to work. This will not only help to create a consistent style, but it will also enable someone else to create pages of a similar format if you were not available.

Before you begin creating your Web pages it is a good idea to write down some guidelines for the production of your pages. These do not have to be rigid rules, but they can be used as a framework around which an effective, and consistent, site can be created. The best way to formulate guidelines is to look at websites and see the elements and styles that you would like to incorporate into your own. Some areas to consider for any guidelines include:

- Fonts. Identify font styles, sizes and colors to be used

- Headings. Specify font, size and colors for main headings and subheadings

- Background color. Specify background colors and patterns to be used, if any

- Format. Specify how the page is going to be formatted i.e. the size and position of tables within the site

- Pixels or percent for tables. This can determine how your Web pages behave when they are resized in a browser window. This can have a considerable impact on the design of a page

- Navigation. Specify how navigation is going to be achieved throughout the site and whether the main navigation is going to consist of horizontal or vertical navigation bars

- Images. Specify details about how images are to be used in relation to their physical size and their file size

- Logos. Decide whether logos are going to be used throughout the site and, if so, specify a consistent size and position

- Additional features. Decide whether your pages are going to contain items such as animations, PDF files or Javascript effects. If so, specify the relevant plug-ins that the users will require to access these features and include information about how to download them

PDF (Portable Document Format) files are ones created with Adobe Acrobat. They retain their original format and design and they can be viewed through a browser with the Acrobat Reader. This is a free plug-in that can be downloaded from the Adobe website at www.adobe.com

A plug-in is a small program that usually enables users to view files In specific formats, such as animations and videos. Most plug-ins are free and they are either pre-installed in browsers or they can be downloaded from the relevant websites.

Creating a site structure

Give folders meaningful names, so that you can quickly identify them if you want to view their contents or create links from other files and folders.

One of the factors that enables all of the pages on the WWW to be connected together, if the authors of them so wish, is the fact that they can be accessed in a specific location on the computer on which they are hosted. In order to conform to this, it is important to create a file structure for your own website before you begin authoring the pages. Initially, this will consist of a new folder or directory, which is known as the root folder, as all of the subsequent folders and files will branch off from it. Once the root folder has been created, sub-folders can then be added. These can contain files for separate sections of your site and also elements such as images and multimedia files that are to be incorporated into the Web pages.

In general, it is best to keep images in the same folder as the document in which they appear. However, this does not mean that they cannot then also appear in other documents which are located in different locations.

When you first begin putting your site together, you may feel it is unnecessary to create a lot of separate folders for different parts of your site. Indeed, it is perfectly possible to include all of the elements of a website within one folder. However, as your site grows you will appreciate the value of creating an ordered and organized site structure.

Links can be made from any file to any other within a site. You just have to know which folder to navigate to in order to make the link. For more information about links see Chapter Three.

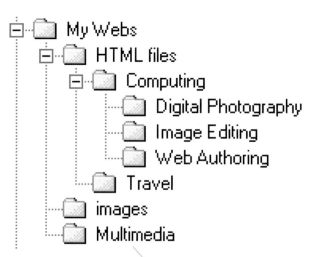

The folder structure for a website could look something like this. (When you come to creating the individual pages, make sure they are saved into the relevant folders within the structure)

Writing for the Web

One of the most common mistakes made when people are preparing text for Web pages is that they think it is just a question of reproducing the same style as they would for a hard copy publication. This is certainly not the case and Web authors should keep the medium for which they are writing firmly at the front of their mind during the authoring process. Some of the ways in which Web publishing differs from the hard copy variety are:

One method that has been developed to make on-screen text easier to read is ebooks and ebook reader software. This is a technique that uses the latest technology in font design to create text that is clearer to read on-screen than traditional font types. This can then be formatted into an ebook, which can be read using the ebook reader software. The two companies at the forefront of this technology are Adobe and Microsoft.

- People find it harder to read text on screen than in hard copy

- For long textual documents on screen it can be frustrating to have to scroll a long way down to read all of the text

- Most users are used to a more visual environment on the Web, rather than just a static textual one

Some of the techniques that can be used to overcome these problems are:

- Rewrite passages of text so that they are shorter and more concise. Get the message across as quickly as possible. This is a good philosophy for most forms of writing, but it is particularly appropriate when writing for the Web

- Use plenty of headings and subheadings. This helps to break up the text and provide the reader with a "road map" of the content of the passage

- Convey important points using numbered lists or bullet points. This will enable the reader to quickly identify the key items in the passage

Using more advanced Web publishing techniques, text can also be displayed through animation and rollover functions. For more information on creating rollovers see Chapter Nine.

- Split up long passages of text by putting them on several pages. These can then be linked by using Next and Previous buttons on subsequent pages

- Include summary information in boxes within the text or in the on-screen margins

The good and the bad

When good and bad examples of how text is used on the Web are viewed together it is clear to see how important it is to take some care and effort when writing for the Web:

An almost guaranteed way of making users flee from your Web page, never to return, is to present small, tightly-packed text that takes up the whole screen and is not broken up in any way.

The text here is far too tightly packed together and there is not enough white space around it. Also, it appears as one large block and is not broken up in any way

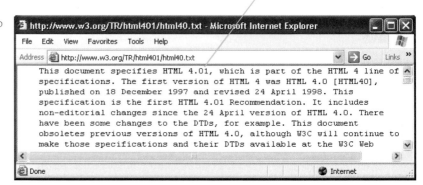

Margins on a page and white space can be created through the use of tables in a HTML document. For more information about creating and using tables, see Chapter Three.

Subheadings and lists break up the text

White space makes the text easier to read

When breaking up text into manageable portions do not be too ruthless and include only a line or two on each page. This may frustrate the reader as they have to keep moving to the next page to read just a sentence or two.

Previous and Next buttons allow the reader to move between manageable portions of text

Download time

Items that take the longest to download are multimedia effects such as animation, sound and video. There are some programs that can produce very effective animations with relatively short downloading times but it is probably best to master static images before this is attempted. Two of these programs are Macromedia Flash and Adobe's GoLive.

When the WWW first became widely available to the general public, people were impressed to just see a few lines of text appear on their computer screens. However, as it has evolved, users have become used to images and an assortment of multimedia effects on their Web pages. This not only means an enhanced user experience, it also means that pages take longer to download onto the user's computer, since they contain a greater amount of information. Despite this, users have become more and more demanding as far as speed of downloading is concerned: they still want the full multimedia experience but they are not prepared to wait too long for it to appear. This increase in user expectation presents a significant challenge for anyone creating Web pages. They have to be able to create pages that are engaging enough so that the users want to keep looking at them, while ensuring that they download quickly enough so that the users do not become bored and move onto another site.

Using images

For a more detailed view of digital photography, have a look at "Digital Photography in easy steps".

Photographic or graphical images are one of the best ways to capture, and keep, people's attention on a website. However, there are some guidelines that should be followed to make these as effective as possible and reduce potential downloading time:

- If possible, resize images before they are placed on a Web page. This means that the images are created at the correct size before they are inserted. This can help reduce the overall size of images and also the downloading time

- Capture digital images at a low resolution. Computer monitors are only capable of displaying a limited number of the colored dots that make up digital images (pixels). This means that digital photographs or scanned images, can be captured at a low resolution, without losing any quality when they are viewed on screen. An image with a low resolution is smaller than one with a higher resolution

Do not create thumbnails too small, or else the user will not be able to make them out properly and so the effect will be wasted.

- Use thumbnails. These are reduced version of the original image. If they are used on a Web page, a hyperlink can be used to allow the user to access a larger version of the image, if they want

Methods for creating pages

Plain HTML

The vast majority of Web pages are created using HyperText Markup Language (HTML), which is a code which instructs a Web browser to display information in a particular way. HTML consists of a variety of tags that are inserted around the text and serve as an instruction for that piece of text. The most basic way to create Web pages is to write the HTML code from scratch. This is not as daunting as it sounds, but it can be time-consuming compared with some of the other methods that are available. HTML code can be created in a text editor, such as NotePad (Windows) or TextEdit (Mac). Once the HTML code has been created in a text editor it looks like this:

See Chapters 2–3 for more information about how to create Web pages using plain HTML code.

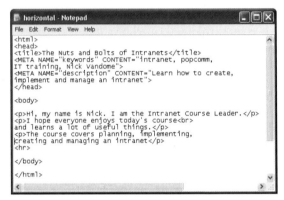

Although the first sight of plain HTML code can be a bit daunting, it is not as complicated as it looks. It is not a full-blown computer language, by a long way, and once the basics have been mastered most people will be able to create Web pages with plain HTML code. This is also known as hand-coding.

For a HTML file to be seen in its graphical format it has to be saved and then viewed through a browser. In the above example this would result in a page that looks like this:

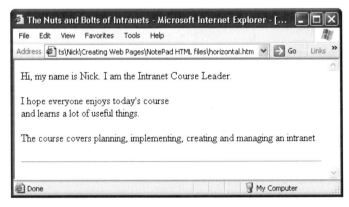

HTML editors

HTML editors are programs that allow Web designers to use plain HTML but they offer the means to insert it more quickly. So rather than having to write every piece of code by hand the designer can select buttons and commands to make the HTML editor do much of the laborious work for them. The designer still has complete control over the appearance of the page, but the HTML editor makes the process more streamlined. A lot of HTML editors can be downloaded for free from the Web and some to look at are:

All HTML editors are slightly different, so try a few out from the Web before you decide on the one that is best for your needs.

* CoffeeCup at www.coffeecup.com

* CuteHTML at www.cuteftp.com

* NoteTab at www.notetab.com

HTML editors create plain HTML code but the interface usually has a range of tools that can be used to help create the code:

HTML editors can be downloaded from the Web at CNET at www.cnet.com

HTML editors create HTML code using tools and icons to make the process as quick and efficient as possible

HTML editors are a good way to learn the basics of HTML coding, without having to type everything from scratch.

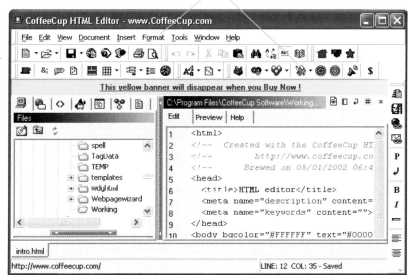

WYSIWYG editors

WYSIWYG is an acronym for What You See Is What You Get and it is a term that is used for Web authoring programs that allow the designer to place all of the items, such as text, graphics and tables, directly on the page in exactly the way they will appear when viewed through a browser. In many ways this type of editor is more closely associated with a desktop publishing program. With a WYSIWYG program the designer does not have to have any knowledge of HTML as the program creates this automatically in the background. However, it is still beneficial to know some HTML as most of these programs have a function for editing the code by hand as well as creating the pages directly with the graphical interface.

Although WYSIWYG editors are one of the quickest and most effective ways of creating Web pages they do have some disadvantages. These include the fact that they sometimes create strange, and unnecessary HTML code and there can be compatibility problems when the pages they create are viewed in different browsers. However, overall they are an excellent way to create Web pages, although some HTML purists may disagree.

Some WYSIWYG program are free and can be downloaded from the Web while others, such as the more professional programs such as Macromedia's Dreamweaver, Adobe's GoLive or Microsoft's FrontPage, are more expensive and start in the range of $100. Although these programs are more expensive than shareware that can be downloaded from the Web, they offer an impressive array of Web authoring tools that can be used to quickly create professional and effective Web pages. For the casual user a free program will be adequate, but anyone else should consider one of the more professional programs.

Online sites

Some websites offer users the means to create their own websites, without leaving the online sites. These are usually done with a variety of templates and wizards. It is a quick way to create functional websites, but it is a little limited in the design options which it offers. Some sites that offer this service include:

Creating Web pages with online services is looked at in more detail in Chapter 5–6.

• Apple's HomePage

• AOL

• Yahoo GeoCities

Publishing a site

Before you publish

Once the hard work of creating a website has been completed you will be desperate to publish it on the Web so that the whole world can see it, or at least your family and friends. Before you do this though it is best to do a few pre-publication checks. These could include:

Web pages should be treated with the same seriousness as any other type of document. There is no excuse for sloppiness and any errors will reflect poorly on the published site.

- Proofreading. Anything that is going to be published on the Web should be spell-checked and given a thorough proofreading: mistakes on Web pages are just as obvious and detrimental as those in hard copy format

- Check overall size. Make sure that the size of your HTML files, images and any multimedia files are not too large as this will have an impact on how quickly the pages of the site download. HTML files tend not to be too large on their own, since they are just made up of text. The areas to watch out for are the images and multimedia files such as animation, video and sound

Most ISPs offer Web space of between 5 to 50 Mb. This is a large amount for a website and should be more than enough for most people. If your website is bigger than this then you should consider some serious editing of it.

- Check hyperlinks. Hyperlinks are the elements of a Web page that allow the user to jump from one page to another (or another area within the same page). If these do not work properly, the user will very quickly become fed up and move on to another site. Check all of these links by viewing the site in a browser and then clicking on each link to make sure it goes to where it is supposed to

Elements of publishing

In order to publish a website, two things are crucial:

Check you ISP's online documentation to see what they offer in the way of Web hosting and Web space.

- Someone to host your site

- A program to enable you to transfer your files from your own computer onto the host's computer

Most companies who offer Internet access – i.e. Internet Services Providers (ISPs) – also provide space on their computers for subscribers to post their own Web pages. If you have an ISP that provides free access to the Internet, then you should be able to publish your Web pages for free too.

Uploading a site

Unless you are using an online Web publishing service, you will need to upload your completed site onto the computer, or server, of the company that is hosting your site. This is usually done with a method called File Transfer Protocol (FTP). Basically this involves copying the files from your local site i.e. your own computer, onto the remote computer where the site will be hosted i.e. your ISP's server.

When uploading a site, make sure you include all of the files that make up the site, including images and multimedia files, and not just the HTML files on their own.

Most professional level Web authoring programs have a method of FTP built into them, but for free or entry level programs an additional FTP program will be required. These can usually be download for free from the Web and some to look at include:

*   WS_FTP at www.ipswitch.com

*   BulletProofFTP at www.bpftp.com

*   CuteFTP at www.cuteftp.com

*   Fetch at http://fetchsoftworks.com (for Mac users)

Some of the FTP settings that may be required to upload a site include:

*   *username*
*   *password*
*   *the name of the computer, or server, where the files are going to be uploaded to*

For more details about uploading files with FTP, see Chapter Eleven.

Once you have obtained an FTP program you can then upload your files onto your ISP's server. This will involve including certain settings to complete the FTP process. These vary from ISP to ISP but most of them have details of this in their help or technical information.

When you upload files you will probably be faced with a screen that shows both the local and the remote locations. During uploading, the files from the local computer should be copied to the remote one. FTP programs have a variety of functions built in to them to make the process as quick and as smooth as possible. However, the main function is transferring files over the Internet from one computer to another. Once the files have been transferred by FTP they are live, i.e. they can be viewed on the Web by anyone who knows the Web address, or URL.

HTML basics

HyperText Markup Language (HTML) is the foundation on which all Web pages are built. This chapter goes over the basics of creating HTML by hand and shows how to begin creating your first Web page.

Covers

Chapter Two

HTML overview

The first thing to say about HyperText Markup Language (HTML) is that it is not a full-blown computer language, in the same mould as the likes of C++ or Javascript. Rather it is a code that uses sets of tags to inform Web browsers how certain items of information should be displayed. These tags are contained within angled brackets and there is usually, but not always, an opening and a closing tag. HTML tags work in a similar way to early word processors, which created formatting such as bold and italics by putting the relevant tags around the items to be formatted. So, if you want to produce bold text on a Web page it would look like this in the HTML file:

Hi. My name is Nick

To open a HTML file on your computer in a browser, open the browser, select File>Open and then Browse to where the HTML file is on your computer. Select it, select Open and then select OK. The file should then be displayed in the browser. Keep this open if you are editing the HTML file, so that you can view the changes.

Creating and viewing HTML files

HTML files are plain text files and they do not contain any actual images or multimedia effects. If these appear on the finished page it is because the HTML file includes a tag that directs the browser to display a certain item on the page at that point. Therefore, if a photograph appears on a Web page, the HTML file will have a reference to where this file is located and how it is to be displayed on the page, rather than the image itself. This is why all files that are required on a Web page have to be uploaded to the host server: the HTML itself does not necessarily contain all of the information that will be displayed on the Web.

When a HTML file has been updated and saved, click the Refresh (Internet Explorer) or Reload (Netscape) button on the browser to view the changes.

HTML files can be created in text editors such as Notepad (Windows) or TextEdit (Mac). When the file is being created, all that will be visible is the text and the HTML tags. However, once the file has been saved it can then be opened via a Web browser, at which point the format of the page will be displayed, along with any images or multimedia effects. HTML files have to be saved with a "–.htm" or a "–.html" file extension. So a default page for a website could be saved as "default.htm". Every time a HTML file is altered it has to be saved before the changes can be viewed through a browser.

Common HTML tags

Some of the most commonly used HTML tags are shown below. They all have corresponding closing tags, unless stated:

HTML is quite forgiving in terms of accuracy of the code that is entered. If tags are missed, or extra ones inserted, the page will still be displayed, although some elements may not look exactly as they should. This is unlike more sophisticated computer languages, such as Javascript, that can refuse to work if even a comma is put in the wrong place or omitted.

- <html>. This appears at the beginning of every HTML document to identify the type of file that it is

- <title>. This gives the file a title that appears when it is viewed in a browser

- <head>. This contains information about the document that is not usually visible on screen

- <body>. This contains the main content of the document

- <p>. This is used to signify a new paragraph

-
. This is used to insert a line break, which creates a smaller gap than the <p> tag. The <br> tag has no corresponding closing tag

- <hr>. This is used to insert a horizontal line. It has no corresponding closing tag

- <a href>. This is used to create a hyperlink within a HTML document. The closing tag is </a>

New versions of HTML appear periodically, which include new tags. For the latest information about HTML developments have a look at the website of the World Wide Web Consortium at: www.w3.org

This contains valuable HTML reference material and also a HTML Validator which can be used to check the accuracy of HTML code.

- <img src>. This is used to specify the location of an image that is to be inserted. It has no closing tag as all of the information is contained within the <img src> tag

- <h1–6>. This is used to create headings at predefined sizes, ranging from 1 (largest) to 6 (smallest)

- <ul>. This creates a bulleted list

- <ol>. This creates a numbered list

- <table>. This is used to insert a table

- <tr>. This used to insert table rows

- <td>. This is used to insert table cells

Head content

The only part of the head content that is visible when the file is viewed through a browser is the Title part. See the facing page for more details.

The head content of a HTML page appears directly after the `<html>` tag. It contains a variety of information that does not appear in the published document but is used to determine certain characteristics of the page and also control some of its functions. Some of the items that could be included in the head content are:

- Meta tags, which can contain keywords that are used by search engines. They can also contain information about the file such as the type of document and any encoding it contains

Meta tags can be used to insert keywords that relate to the page, or site, that is being published. These are then used by search engines to determine whether the file matches a particular search. Keywords are usually placed in the meta tags on the home page of a website i.e. the first page that users see when they access the site. Keywords appear in the format, "Meta name="Keywords" content= "X, Y, Z"

- Scripts such as Javascript or VBScript. These can be used to control any scripts that appear in the file

- Style definitions. These are generally in the form of Cascading Style Sheets (CSS) that are used to apply set attributes to a whole page at a time

The head content of a file can include all, or none, of the above items. If head content has been added to a HTML file it would look something like this:

```
<head>

<META NAME="keywords" CONTENT="intranet, popcomm,
IT training, Nick Vandome>

<META NAME="description">

<style type="text/css">

<!--

.text {  font-family: Arial, Helvetica, sans-
serif; font-size: 14px; text-decoration: none}

-->

</style>

</head>
```

Cascading Style Sheets are an advanced HTML technique that can be used to manipulate the format of an entire page. The formatting is contained within the Cascading Style Sheet and if this is edited, then the appearance of all affected items on the page will also change.

Adding a title

A title in a HTML page is the one part of the head content that is visible when the page is published. However, the title does not appear in the published document itself, but at the top of the browser window. It is usually a description of what appears on the page and it can either be a single word, or a longer sentence. When the title is added to a HTML document it looks like this:

Make sure that every page of a website is given a title. If it is not titled then the title will appear as "Untitled document" in the browser.

The title appears here as part of the head content

```
<html>

<head>

<title>The Nuts and Bolts of Intranets</title>

<META NAME="keywords" CONTENT="intranet, popcomm,
IT training, Nick Vandome>
```

When the HTML page is the viewed through a browser, the title appears here:

Titles in HTML documents are used by some search engines as part of the criteria for their searches. This is one reason why it is important to include titles in documents.

Body content

The body part of a HTML document is everything that appears between the <body> and </body> tags.

The body content of a HTML document is the part that contains all of the content that will be visible when viewed through a browser. This includes text, images and multimedia elements (although the latter two are not contained within the HTML documents, they have a reference to let the browser know where to locate them.) In addition, the body portion of a document can also contain information specifying elements such as background color, plain text color and also the color for text when it is converted into hyperlinks.

If you wanted to specify a black background with white text for a HTML page then the body content in the authoring file would look like this:

```
<body bgcolor="000000" text="FFFFFF">

<p>Hi, my name is Nick. I am the Intranet Course
Leader.</p>
```

When this is viewed through a browser the body content code will be interpreted like this:

It is possible to enter body content into a HTML document without using the <body> tag. However, this should be avoided as it does not allow the same versatility for formatting elements of the page.

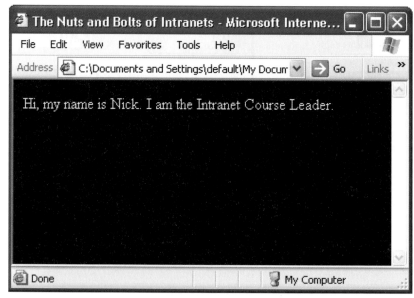

Since the body content of a HTML document can contain such a variety of items, the code within the body can be similarly varied. The following is typical for the type of code that can be used to create a Web page:

```
<table width="764" border="0" cellspacing="2"
cellpadding="2" align="center">
  <tr>
    <td valign="top" height="129">
      <table width="100%" border="0"
cellspacing="2" cellpadding="2">
        <tr>
          <td width="11%" valign="top">
            <p><a href="../INDEX.HTM"><img
src="../popcomm-logo.gif" width="60" height="60"
align="middle" alt="Popcomm logo" border="0"></
a></p>
```

The body text of HTML pages can be very simple (just a few lines of plain text) or it can be fairly complicated. Usually, the more elements on a page, then the more involved the body content will be.

The body code (and the rest of the code too) of HTML files on the Web can be viewed by selecting View>Source from the browser toolbar (Internet Explorer). This then displays the HTML code in a text file. This is a good way to work out how certain styles of pages are constructed.

When this is viewed through a browser the body content code will be interpreted like this:

Paragraph breaks

When entering text into a Web page, one of the primary requirements is the ability to include paragraph breaks and line breaks, in the same way as if you were using a word processor. In HTML, paragraph breaks are achieved with the <p> tag. The text is included after this tag and then the paragraph is ended with the </p> tag. A paragraph break inserts a break that is approximately two lines in size, which gives it the appearance of double spacing. To achieve paragraph breaks the following code could be used:

<p> tags should be used whenever you want to start a new line or paragraph of text.

```
<body>

<p>Hi, my name is Nick. I am the Intranet Course
Leader.</p>

<p>I hope everyone enjoys today's course and
learns a lot of useful things.</p>

<p>The course covers planning, implementing,
creating and managing an intranet</p>

</body>
```

<p> tags can have additional formatting options inserted inside the tag, which will only be applied to that specific paragraph. For instance, if you want to change the text color for a single paragraph, this can be done by inserting more code within the <p> tag.

When this is viewed through a browser, the paragraph breaks will be interpreted like this:

Some elements of HTML, such as the code used for headings, can overwrite any <p> tags, since they have their own paragraph breaks incorporated into that specific tag.

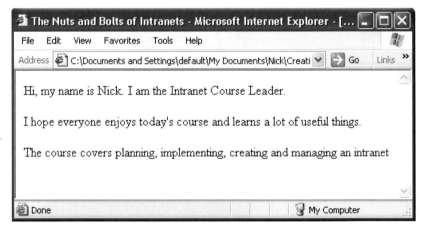

Line breaks

Line breaks are similar to paragraph breaks, except they insert a break of a single line. Also, text inserted after a line break is still in the same paragraph as any preceding text and so it retains the formatting attributes of that paragraph. Line breaks can be used to place text on the next immediate line below any preceding text. A line break tag is <br> and it has no corresponding closing tag. To create formatting with both paragraph breaks and line breaks the following code could be used:

```
<body>

<p>Hi, my name is Nick. I am the Intranet Course
Leader.</p>

<p>I hope everyone enjoys today's course<br>

and learns a lot of useful things.</p>

<p>The course covers planning, implementing,
creating and managing an intranet</p>

</body>
```

Unlike paragraph breaks, line breaks cannot have additional formatting attributes added inside them.

When this is viewed through a browser the paragraph breaks and line breaks will be interpreted like this:

Line breaks can be used to group items closely together, without creating the double spacing effect that occurs with paragraph breaks. This can be useful for items such as lists, although there are also specific tags for creating bulleted and numbered lists in HTML. See page 37 for more details.

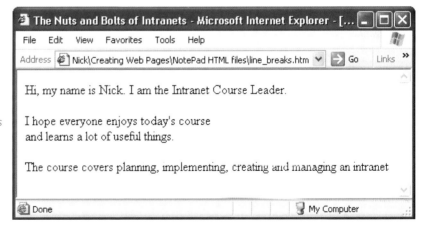

Horizontal lines

Horizontal rules are an excellent way to break up long passages of text in a HTML document and also add valuable white space to the layout and format. This is very important for Web pages as users do not like being confronted by large blocks of unbroken text. Other ways to break up text include the use of headings and sub-headings and bulleted or numbered lists.

HTML has limited scope for adding horizontal lines and this is done with the <hr> tag. This creates a horizontal line which crosses the whole page. This can then be modified in length by including additional instructions within the <hr> tag. The <hr> tag does not have a corresponding closing tag. The following code would insert a horizontal line across an entire page:

```
<p>The course covers planning, implementing,
creating and managing an intranet</p>

<hr>
```

The following code would insert a horizontal line at a specific size:

```
<p>The course covers planning, implementing,
creating and managing an intranet</p>

<hr width=50%>
```

For greater versatility for including horizontal lines, graphics can be used rather than the <hr> tag. The line is created as an image and this is then inserted into the page. This enables you to create more varied styles than allowed by the <hr> tag.

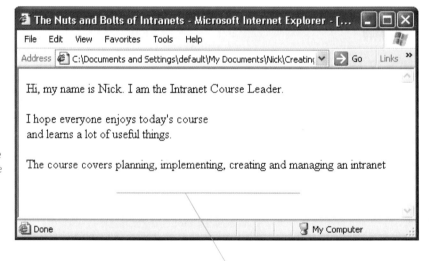

When this is viewed through a browser the horizontal line will be interpreted like this

Fonts and text size

Web pages are more effective with a sans serif (without loops) font, such as Arial or Helvetica, rather than a serif one such as TimesNewRoman. This is because sans serif fonts are made up of more uniform strokes, which are easier to read onscreen.

Unless specified otherwise, text in a HTML document is displayed in a default font and default size. How this is displayed depends on the default settings of the browser in which the file is being viewed, but it is usually TimesNewRoman font at size 3 (this is equivalent to point size 12 in a word processor). This is far from ideal, particularly as TimesNewRoman is not the best font for Web pages. In order to change the font, additional tags have to be added before the text is entered. This can be used to specify a particular font and size at which the text will be displayed when viewed in a browser. The following code contains specific attributes for text within a document:

```
<body><font face="arial">

<p><font size="5"><b>Hi, my name is Nick. I am the
Intranet Course Leader.</font></b></p>

<p><font size="3">I hope everyone enjoys today's
course  and learns a lot of useful things.</font>
</p>

<p><font size="2">The course covers planning,
implementing, creating and managing an intranet</
font></p>

</body>
```

Text formatting attributes can be added into the <body> tag, or they can be applied to a specific piece of text within a document. If this is done, it overrides any formatting options that have been applied within the <body> tag.

When this is viewed through a browser the formatted text will be interpreted like this:

Fonts that have been specified will only be displayed properly if the user has them installed on their computer. Therefore, try not to use any unusual or obscure fonts. If you are in any doubt, include a font family in the code. This means that if one font is not found, the next one on the list will be searched for.

Text color

Different browsers display some hexadecimal colors differently from others. However, there are 256 hexadecimal colors, known as Web-safe colors, that appear the same on any browser. Most professional Web authoring programs use these colors by default and it is worth bearing in mind when adding colors to your own site.

If you want to find out the hexadecimal values for certain colors on the Web, look at the source code and then note down the hexadecimal value for the required colors. Particularly with large corporate sites, it is reasonable to assume that these will be Web-safe.

Colors in HTML documents are specified by hexadecimal values. This is a combination of 6 alphanumeric characters that the browser uses to display the required color. Hexadecimal colors are made up of numbers from 0–6 and letters from A–F. So black would be denoted by 000000 and white would be denoted by FFFFFF. All HTML colors are denoted in this way, regardless of whether they are text colors, background colors or table cell colors.

Text color can be specified for all of the text that appears on a page. To do this the coding for text color appears in the <body> tag:

```
<body text="00AA33">

<p>Hi, my name is Nick. I am the Intranet Course
Leader.</p>

</body>
```

However, if you want to specify a color for a particular piece of text within a document, the coding has to be inserted around the item that is going to have its color changed. It also has to have a closing tag at the point where you want the specified color to end:

```
<body>

<p><font face="arial" font color="0000FF">Hi, my
name is Nick. I am the Intranet Course Leader.</
font></p>

</body>
```

If an individual piece of text has had a color applied to it, this will override any text color that has been set for the whole page within the <body> tag.

Headings

HTML has a number of tags that can be used to create headings in predefined styles. This is done with the <h> tag. This is used in conjunction with the numbers 1–6 to specify the size of a heading. An <h1> tag creates the largest heading and an <h6> tag creates the smallest one. Headings are a useful way to break up large amounts of text and several levels of headings can be used within the same page. The code for this would look like this:

Use headings to display hierarchical information i.e. the largest heading for the most important information and the smallest for the least important.

```
<body>

<h1><font face="arial" font color="0000FF">Hi, my
name is Nick. I am the Intranet Course Leader.</
h1></font>

<h2>I hope everyone enjoys today's course<br>

and learns a lot of useful things.</h2>

<h4>The course covers planning, implementing,
creating and managing an intranet</h4>

<hr>

</body>
```

If additional tags, such as <font size="??">, are inserted in between a heading tag and the text, then this will override the heading tag. However, formatting tags such as <b> for bold or <i> for italics have no effect if they are inserted between the <h> tag and the text: the text still just takes the attributes of the <h> tag.

When this is viewed through a browser the heading tags will be interpreted like this:

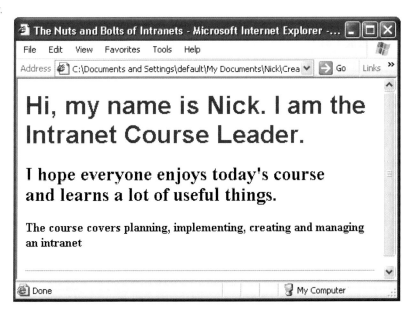

Aligning text

HTML text cannot be justified using the text alignment option shown here.

As with a word processor, text in a HTML document can be aligned on the page, to either the left, centre or right. This is done with the <div> tag which is a relatively new HTML convention for aligning text. Text has to be in a separate paragraph for it to have specific alignment attributes attached to it. If an alignment attribute is assigned to a piece of text that comes after a line break, the whole of the attached paragraph will have this alignment applied to it. Different paragraphs can have different alignment attributes given to them and the code for this would look like this:

```
<body><font face="arial">

<p align="left">Hi, my name is Nick. I am the
Intranet Course Leader.</p>

<p align="center">I hope everyone enjoys today's
course</p>

<p align="right">The course is about intranets</p>

</body>
```

Text can be indented by using the <blockquote> tag. This can be applied to a whole paragraph by inserting this tag at the beginning of the paragraph and a closing </blockquote> tag at the end of the paragraph. Elements within a paragraph cannot be indented separately from the rest of the paragraph.

When this is viewed through a browser the text alignment will be interpreted like this:

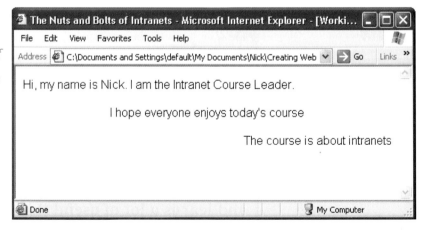

Lists

With the opening list tags, each list item is contained with <li> and </li> tags. This is the same for unordered lists and ordered lists.

Both bulleted and numbered lists can be created in HTML and these are known as unordered and ordered lists respectively. An unordered list uses the <ul> tag and an ordered list uses the <ol> tag. HTML code for unordered and ordered lists looks like this (the unordered list is the first one):

```
<p>The course covers
<ul><li>planning</li>
   <li>implementing</li>
   <li>creating</li>
   <li>managing</li>
</ul>
<p>The two main objectives of the course are:
<ol><li>Commonsense approach</li>
<li>Providing the means to do the job</li>
</ol>
```

Lists are an excellent way of breaking up large blocks of text. This is particularly important for reading text from a computer monitor since people generally find this more tiring than reading from paper. Use bullet points to display lists that have no hierarchical order, or to emphasis certain parts of a document. Use numbered lists for items that have increasing, or decreasing, levels of importance.

When this is viewed through a browser the lists will be interpreted like this:

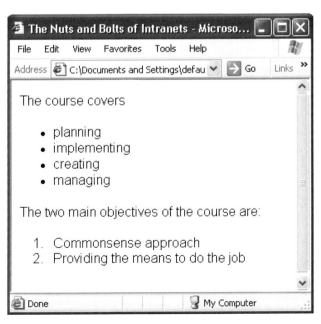

List items can only be created from elements in separate paragraphs: items separated by a line break cannot be made into different list items.

Background color

The background color of a HTML page can be set in a similar way to setting the color for text. The code for background color is specified within the <body> tag. The HTML code for setting background color looks like this (in this example the background color will appear as light green):

Most people experiment with colored backgrounds when they begin designing Web pages. However, this should be used carefully as overly bright backgrounds can be off-putting, particularly when they are being viewed for a long period of time.

```
<body bgcolor="66FFCC">

<h1><font face="arial" font color="0000FF">Hi, my
name is Nick. I am the Intranet Course Leader.</
h1></font>

<h2><font face="arial">I hope everyone enjoys
today's course<br>

and learns a lot of useful things.</h2>
```

When this is viewed through a browser the background color will be interpreted like this:

Always make sure that there is a good contrast between background color and text color. One of the most effective colors for a Web page is white.

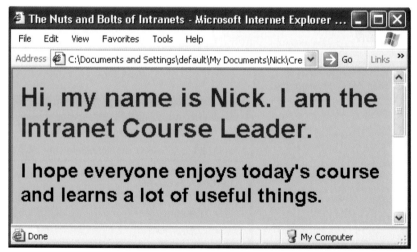

Even if you are using white as a background color, specify this within the <body> tag in the form of <body bgcolor="FFFFFF">. If no background color is specified, browsers will use their default background color, which in some cases is gray.

More HTML

This chapter goes beyond basic HTML functions and shows how to insert and format images and add hyperlinks. It also introduces the fundamentals of two important formatting devices, tables and frames.

Covers

Chapter Three

Using images

Images on the Web

Most Web pages benefit from the inclusion of images, but only if they are used properly. In general, images on Web pages should be:

- Used for a specific purpose, not just to show off

- Be reasonably small on the screen, so that there is enough room for other items

- Be reasonably small in terms of file size, so that they do not increase downloading time too much

Professional image editing programs such as Fireworks and Photoshop can be used to optimize images for the Web i.e. reduce their file size while still retaining an acceptable quality. If you are going to be using a lot of images on the Web, then it would be a good idea to buy some type of image editing program.

When images were first being used on the Web, designers realized that there was a requirement for images that could be compressed in size, while still retaining a good quality. This resulted in the creation of three image formats, that are now primarily used on the Web:

- GIF. This stands for Graphical Interchange Format and is an image format that uses 256 colors and can be greatly compressed without losing much image quality. Because of the relatively small number of colors used in GIFs they are generally best used for graphics that do not have a lot of color variation in terms of tone and shading

Although GIFs may seem restricted in the types of images that they can display, due to the fact that they can only display 256 colors, they are actually surprisingly efficient at dealing with photographic images.

- JPEG. This stands for Joint Photographic Experts Group and can display up to 16 million colors. Because of this, it is generally used for photographic images, although it can also be used for graphical images

- PNG. This stands for Portable Network Group and although it is not as common as GIFs or JPEGs it offers an excellent compromise between compression and quality and it can be used for photographic or graphical images

PNGs are sometimes less compatible with older browsers than GIFs or JPEGs. However, more recent browsers have no problem in displaying them accurately.

One aspect of using images on the Web relates to graphical images that are created with blocks of color. Problems can arise because different browsers interpret different colors in different ways. This has led to the creation of the Web-safe color palette. This is a list of 256 colors that will be displayed in the same way in all browsers.

Inserting images

Images are not inserted directly into a HTML document: a reference is inserted that instructs the browser where to locate the image and it can also contain details about where the image is to be positioned. The following piece of code would instruct a browser to display an image within the HTML document (in this example, the image will be displayed at its original size):

```
<body>
<p><font face="arial" size="5">
<font color="#0000FF"><b>Hi, my name is Nick. I am
the Intranet Course Leader.</b></font></p>
<img src="Nick Vandome3.jpg">
</body>
```

When this is viewed through a browser the image will be appear like this:

Always save the HTML document before you add the <img src> tag. Otherwise the file will not have a point from which to reference itself in relation to the location of the image file.

In this example the image and the HTML file are both contained within the same folder. This means that the <img src> tag can be referenced directly to the file. However, if the image were in a different folder then this would have to be included in the path to the image. This requires the same notation as for creating links to other HTML files. For more details about this, see page 45.

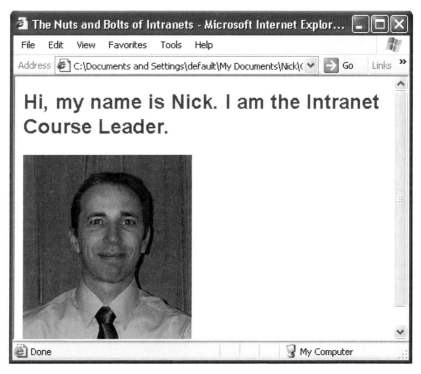

Formatting images

Images can be resized in an image editing program before they are included in a Web page, or they can be resized within the HTML code itself. This can result in an inferior image quality but it is the only option if no additional software is available: The following code can be used within the <img src> tag to specify a size at which the browser is to display a specific image:

```
<body>

<p><font face="arial" size="5">

<font color="#0000FF"><b>Hi, my name is Nick. I am
the Intranet Course Leader.</b></font></p>

<img src="Nick Vandome3.jpg" width="300"
height="330" alt="Nick Vandome, intranet course
leader">

</body>
```

Resizing images with the Height and Width commands can result in them becoming misshapen i.e. their height and width sizes are not maintained in the same proportions as the original.

When this is viewed through a browser the image will be appear like this (if the height and width code were removed then the image would revert to its original size, i.e. the size at which it is displayed on the previous page):

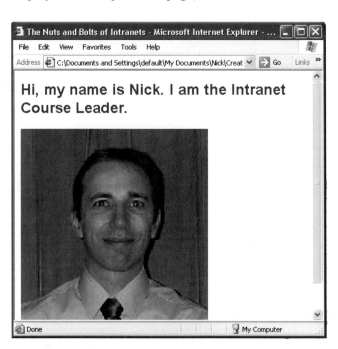

Graphical WYSIWYG (What You See Is What You Get) Web authoring tools allow you to resize images by clicking on them and dragging, in the same way as you would with an image in a word processing or desktop publishing program. Hold down Shift to maintain proportions when the image is being resized with dragging.

Aligning images

Images can be aligned in the same way as text: to the left, right or centre. The following code shows how a single image can be presented at different sizes and aligned at various point of a page:

```
<p><font face="arial" size="5">

<font color="#0000FF"><b>Hi, my name is Nick. I am
the Intranet Course Leader.</b></font></p>

<p align="center"><img src="Nick Vandome3.jpg"
width="300" height="330" alt="Nick Vandome"></p>

<p align="left"><img src="Nick Vandome3.jpg"
width="100" height="110" alt="Nick Vandome"></p>
```

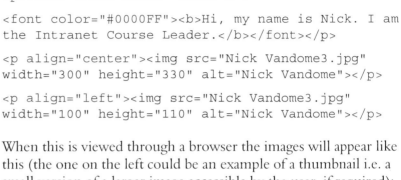

The best way to position images within a HTML page is to place them within a table. Tables are looked at in greater detail on page 51.

When this is viewed through a browser the images will appear like this (the one on the left could be an example of a thumbnail i.e. a small version of a larger image accessible by the user, if required):

About hyperlinks

URL stands for Uniform Resource Locator and it refers to the unique address of every page on the Web.

Without hyperlinks (or just links), the Web would be an unconnected collection of pages and sites that would be tortuous to navigate around since you would have to specify the Web address (URL) for each page that you wanted to view. Hyperlinks simplify this process considerably: they are pieces of HTML coding that create "clickable" regions on a Web page i.e. the user can click on a hyperlink and it will take them to the linked item. In simple terms, hyperlinks are shortcuts for jumping between elements on the Web.

Both text and images can be used as hyperlinks: text usually appears underlined when it is acting as a hyperlink and, for both elements, the cursor turns into a pointing hand when it is positioned over a hyperlink on a Web page. If you click at this point you will be taken to the linked item. Some of the items that hyperlinks can be linked to are:

If you are using images as hyperlinks, make sure that they are clearly identifiable, otherwise the user may think they are just a graphical design feature.

- Other pages within the same website

- Other locations within the same page

- Other websites

- Email addresses

Hyperlinks to other Web pages are created by using the <a href=> tag, which is closed by inserting the </a> tag. So the code for a simple hyperlink to a page within the same site structure could look like:

<a href="news.htm">Latest News</a>

In this example the words "Latest News" would be underlined on the page and when the user clicks on them, the page "news.htm" will open.

Document-relative links

Depending on the type of link that is being created, the address that you use as the link will vary. For instance, if you are linking to a page within your own site, this is called a document-relative link and if you are linking to another site on the Web, this is called an absolute link.

The other type of link is an absolute link. This is one that goes externally to another page on the Web i.e. one that is stored on another server. This means that the full URL has to be inserted so the browser viewing the pages knows where to look.

An absolute path for a Web page is always prefixed with "http://" and then followed by the address of the page.

A document-relative link to a file within the same structure and in the same folder would have a link straight to the file name i.e. <a href="main.htm">My Day</a>. This is the simplest type of link to insert and, if possible, it is preferable to try and use this format as much as possible.

If you want to link to a file in a sub-folder of the one in which your source folder is located, then the link would look like this:

<a href="events/main.htm">My Day</a>

If these two files were linked, the hyperlink code would be as above

The notation "../" in a hyperlink address means move up one level in the folder hierarchy and "/" means move down one level. This acts as an instruction to the browser viewing a page as to where to look for the linked file.

If your site structure consists of several different levels of folders, your links can become quite complicated.

If you want to link to a file in the main (or parent) folder to the one in which your source folder is located, then the link would look like this:

<a href="../birthday.htm">Celebrate</a>

If these two files were linked, the hyperlink code would be as above

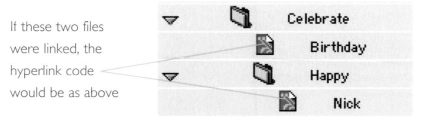

Adding hyperlinks

Both text and images can be made into hyperlinks and in both cases the <a href> tag is used. The closing tag for this is </a> which is inserted after the code for the hyperlink and also the element that is being used as the link. This creates a hyperlink that will take the user to a different page within the site, or to a different site altogether.

By default, text that is converted into a hyperlink is colored blue and appears underlined. This can be changed by using a device called a Cascading Style Sheet, which defines the attributes for all of the elements on a page, or just a single one.

Textual links

For a piece of text to be converted into a hyperlink the code would look like this:

```
<body>
<p><font face="arial" size="3">
<a href="index.htm">Back to intranet home page
</a></p>
<p><font face="arial" size="5">Hi, my name is
Nick. I am the Intranet Course Leader.</font></p>
```

When this is viewed through a browser the textual hyperlink will appear like this:

Textual hyperlinks can be colored differently depending on their current state i.e. before they have been activated, when they are being clicked on and once they have been activated (visited). The colors for each of these states for the whole page can be specified within the <body> tag and the code would look like this: <body link="#99FF66" vlink="#FFFF00" alink="#33FFFF">

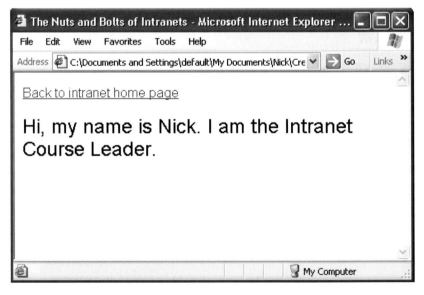

Image links

Images can be used as hyperlinks in a similar way to text. However, make sure that it is clear to the user that the image is the link, otherwise they may not realize that they have to click on it. If necessary, add a short textual description to explain that an image is a link and where it will take the user once they click on it. By default, image links do not have a border, but one can be added within the code.

All images on a website should have an ALT tag attached to them. This is a piece of text that is visible when the cursor is placed over an image. This provides a brief description of the page and also enables users with impaired vision to discover the contents of the image through a special device that reads the contents of the ALT tag.

Also, if users have their browsers set so that images are not displayed, the ALT tag shows them what they are missing. In this example an ALT tag has been added to the image in the form of: alt="Nick Vandome, intranet course leader" which appears within the <img src> tag.

For an image to be converted into a hyperlink the code would look like this (this includes a one point size border around the image):

```
<p><font face="arial" size="3">

<a href="index.htm">Back to intranet home page
</a></p>

<p><font face="arial" size="5">Hi, my name is
Nick. I am the Intranet Course Leader.</font></p>

<p align="center"><a href="index.htm"><img
src="Nick Vandome3.jpg" width="200" height="220"
border="2" alt="Nick Vandome, intranet course
leader"></a></p>
```

When this is viewed through a browser the image hyperlink will appear like this:

A textual description can also be applied to a textual hyperlink, in the same way as an ALT tag can be added to an image. This is done by substituting the ALT tag with the TITLE tag.

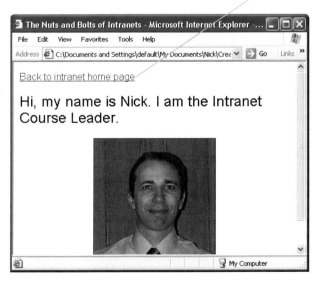

Anchors

Anchors are a device where a hyperlink is used to link two points within the same page, rather than linking to another page or site. This involves inserting two pieces of HTML code; one for the anchor point and another for the hyperlink that will take the user to the anchor. Anchors are usually used for long Web pages, since on smaller pages the user can see most of the information on a single screen and there is no need to include an anchor to another part of the page.

If possible, try and keep Web pages to a reasonable size, so that the user does not have to scroll a long way down to see all of the information. Long textual documents can be broken up by putting them onto separate pages and then adding Next and Previous buttons to each page so that users can navigate between them. If a lot of information has to be included on a single page, then anchors are one way to allow users to navigate quickly around he information.

The following would be how an anchor would be displayed in HTML code:

```
<body>

<a name="top"></a>

<p><font face="arial" size="3">

<a href="index.htm">Back to intranet home page</a>
</p>
```

See below for the relevant hyperlink:

If an anchor point takes the user to another point of a long Web page, make sure that you include a Back to Top button at the point where the anchor occurs. This is done by inserting another anchor at the top of the page and then inserting a link to it from the vicinity of the anchor further down the page. This then gives the user the means to move quickly up and down the page.

```
<p>The two main objectives of the course are:

<ol>

<li>Commonsense approach</li>

<li>Providing the means to do the job</li>

</ol>

<a href="#top">Back to top</a>

</body>
```

The code for the hyperlink connecting to the anchor point would look like this

When the anchor point and the hyperlink are viewed through a browser they will appear like this:

Anchors are a good device to use when there are a lot of natural breaks in a document, such as long lists or articles that have a lot of headings and subheadings.

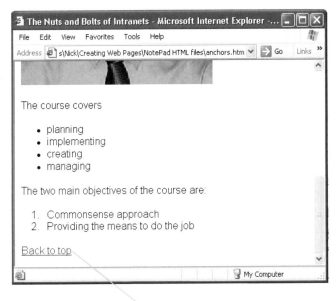

Anchors can also be used to link to a specific point in another page or website. To do this, insert an anchor in the target page and then insert a hyperlink in the page which is going to link to the anchor. The code for the hyperlink will look like this: <a href="My Doc.htm#anchor">Move to anchor point</a>

When the user clicks on the hyperlink here, they are taken to the anchor point at the top of the page

Anchors are not visible when viewed on the published page.

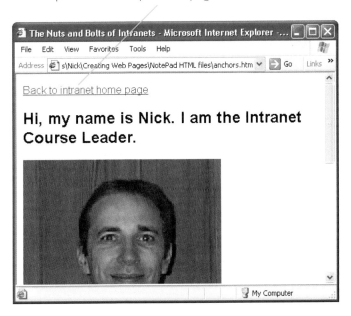

Formatting hyperlinks

Textual hyperlinks can be formatted in the same way as other pieces of text in a HTML document. This includes font, size and color, although the latter will be displayed as the default color unless specified otherwise. The colors for the different states of a hyperlink can also be specified in the <body> tag. The following is an example of the type of code that can be used to format a textual hyperlink (this includes the code within the <body> tag that specifies the colors for the different states of the hyperlink):

```
<body link="006633" vlink="990033" alink="00CCFF">
<p><font face="century gothic" size="5"><i>
<a href="index.htm">Back to intranet home page
</a></i></p>
<p><font face="arial" size="5">Hi, my name is
Nick. I am the Intranet Course Leader.</font></p>
```

The different states for a textual hyperlink are: Normal, which is how the hyperlink appears in a browser before it has been clicked; Active, which is how the hyperlink appears in a browser while it is in the process of being clicked; and Visited, which is how the hyperlink appears once it has been clicked and the user then returns to the same page.

When viewed in a browser the formatted hyperlink will appear like this:

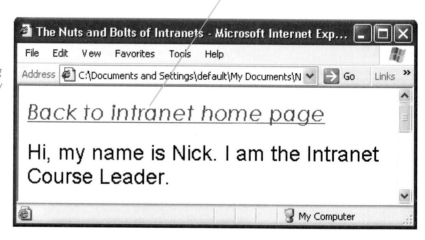

Tables

Think of tables as containers into which HTML content can be placed and then formatted.

Despite their name, tables in HTML are not just for displaying mathematical or financial data. They can handle this task with ease, but they are also extremely versatile in that they can contain text, images and even multimedia elements. In fact, any element that can be used in a HTML page can also be inserted into a table.

One of the greatest benefits of tables in HTML is for positioning elements more accurately than can be done by using the HTML commands such as align left, center or right. Instead a table can be inserted into a page and this can then be formatted with numerous rows and columns. Content can then be added to the individual cells and so complex designs can be created, with each element positioned with great accuracy.

Tables are probably the single most useful design feature for positioning items on a page. Unless you are going to just be designing very simple pages, consider inserting tables before you add any other content onto the page.

Tables are created with the <table> tag and a considerable amount of additional code can also be added to format the table. The following code is for inserting a table that contains a single cell i.e. one row and one column (the table also has an image inserted):

```
<table width="100%" border="2">
        <tr>
            <td><img src="Nick Vandome3.jpg"></td>
        </tr>
</table>
```

When viewed in a browser the table will appear like this:

Most professional websites use tables in their design. Some use complex table formats to create pages that look more like they have been created in a desktop publishing program. This shows the power and versatility of using tables.

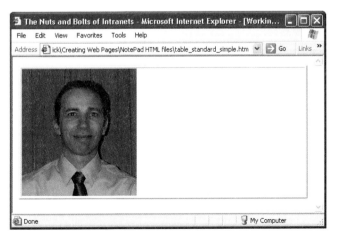

Headers can be inserted into tables by using the <thead> tag. This occurs directly after the <table> tag and results in the information contained within it being formatted as a heading, usually in bold. Within the <thead> tag <tr> tags can be used to specify the number of rows to which the heading applies and the <th> tag can be used in place of the <td> tag in the main part of the table.

Footers can also be added in a similar way by using the <tfoot> tag.

Adding rows and columns

The number of rows and columns in a table is determined by the <tr> and <td> tags. The <tr> tag determines the number of rows in a table and the <td> tag determines the number of cells within a row, which in effect sets the number of columns. If all of the rows and columns in a table are symmetrical then each row will have the same number of cells. However, it is possible to vary the size of each cell and even merge adjoining cells together. The code for a table with multiple rows and columns would look like this:

```
<table width="500" border="1">
    <tr>
      <td>One</td>
      <td>Two</td>
      <td>Three</td>
      <td>Four</td>
    </tr>
    <tr>
      <td>Five</td>
      <td>Six</td>
      <td>Seven</td>
      <td>Eight</td>
    </tr>
</table>
```

Make sure that each table row has the correct number of cells. If not, some of the cells may appear incomplete when viewed in a browser.

When viewed in a browser the table will appear like this:

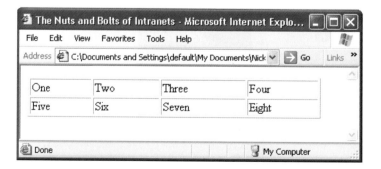

Formatting rows and columns

Columns and rows can be formatted in a variety of ways, to create complex and asymmetrical designs. This is done by changing the sizes of specific cells and also merging them together. This involves specifying a size for a cell and using the <colspan> tag to merge adjoining cells. The following code is for a table where the cells on the top row have been created at four equal sizes and the ones on the bottom row have been merged to form two individual cells:

```
<table width="500" border="1" cellspacing="4"
cellpadding="4" bordercolor="CC9900"
bgcolor="FFFFCC">
  <tr>
    <td><p align="center"><b>One</b></td>
    <td><p align="center"><b>Two</b></td>
    <td><p align="center"><b>Three</b></td>
    <td><p align="center"><b>Four</b></td>
  </tr>
  <tr>
    <td colspan="2" valign="top">
      <p align="center"><b>Five</b></td>
    <td colspan="2" valign="top">
      <p align="center"><b>Six</b></td>
  </tr>
</table>
```

Professional Web authoring programs such as Dreamweaver, GoLive and FrontPage are excellent for creating and editing tables automatically.

If a table cell does not contain any content it may not be visible when the table is viewed in a browser. One way around this is to include a non-breaking space in the cell. This is done by inserting the   in a cell, between the <td> tag and the </td> tag. This does not appear in the browser, but it will make the cell visible.

When viewed in a browser the table will appear like this:

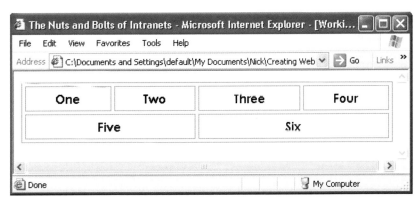

If setting the width in percent, make it smaller than 100%, so that there is some white space around the content.

A pixel is a tiny dot used to display digital information on a computer monitor.

There are advantages and disadvantages with both methods of sizing tables, but most professional Web designers favor setting the width to an absolute size (i.e. a pixel size). This is because it preserves the integrity of the page design no matter the size of monitor or window on which it is being viewed.

Percent or pixels

By default, if no width size is specified for a table, it will appear in the whole window when it is viewed in a browser i.e. it takes up 100% of the browser window. This can be modified so that it takes up a smaller, or larger, proportion of the browser window e.g. 50% or 120% of the window. This is a common design feature, as it is useful to have some white space around content on a page as this can make it easier for the user to read and interpret.

However, as well as setting the width of a table as a percentage of the browser window, it is also possible to specify an absolute size by setting the width in pixels. This means that the table will always appear at this size, regardless of the size of the browser window. One of the main differences in these two methods occurs when the browser window is resized. If the width is set as a percentage the whole of the page will remain on screen if the window is minimized. However, this means that the page design could be altered to fit everything on. Alternatively, if the width is set as an absolute size, the formatting will remain the same, although the whole page may not fit in the browser window so the scroll bars may need to be used to see the whole page.

Percent

The code for a table width set as a percent would look like this:

```
<table width="65%" border="2">
        <tr>
            <td><img src="Nick Vandome3.jpg"></td>
        </tr>
</table>
```

If no width size is specified for a table it will default to 100%.

Individual cells can also have their width set as a percent of the whole table or as an absolute pixels size.

When viewed in a browser the table will appear like this:

A table with one row and one column i.e. a single cell can be used as a container for all of the rest of the content on a page.

If an item, such as an image, that is bigger than the table, is inserted then the table will expand to accommodate it.

As a general guide a table set to 950 pixels wide will take up most of the width of a 17" monitor.

If the width of a table is set in pixels, only the numerical value needs to be included e.g. width="750". The fact that it is in pixels is automatically interpreted by the browser.

The table takes up the specified percentage of the browser window, regardless of the size of the window

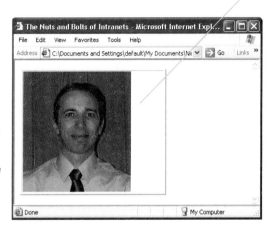

Pixels

The code for a table width set in pixels would look like this:

```
<table width="500" border="1" cellspacing="4"
cellpadding="4" bordercolor="CC9900"
bgcolor="FFFFCC">
```

When viewed in a browser the table will appear like this:

The table retains its absolute pixel size, regardless of the size of the browser window. This can mean that scrollbars are needed to see all of a table set to a pixel width

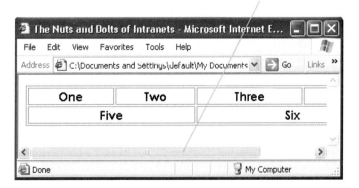

Borders

By default, HTML tables have a border around the outer edges of the table and also all of the cells within it. This is displayed at a line weight of 1. However, it is possible to specify a specific border size and also produce a table where no border is visible. This is particularly useful if you want to produce a complex design that does not look as if it is contained within a table. In the following example, the code for the table includes a border of weight 4. (To create a table with no border, set the border value to 0.)

Make sure you include content if your table has a border value of 0. Otherwise there may be nothing visible when the table is viewed in a browser.

```
<table width="75%" border="4">
    <tr>
       <td>One</td>
       <td>Two</td>
       <td>Three</td>
       <td>Four</td>
    </tr>
    <tr>
       <td>Five</td>
       <td>Six</td>
       <td>Seven</td>
       <td>Eight</td>
    </tr>
</table>
```

Tables that have been produced without a border can create an effect similar to a design with a desktop publishing program for a hard copy publication.

When viewed in a browser the table will appear like this:

Table borders can also have colors applied to them. This is done by inserting this line of code: <table border="1" bordercolor="#0000FF">. In this example the border will consist of a weight of 1 and be colored blue. This includes the outer border of the table and all of the cells.

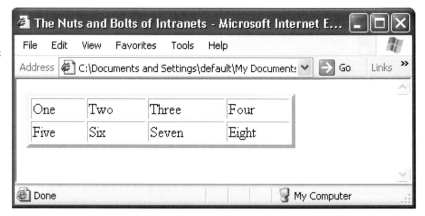

Cell spacing and cell padding can be applied independently of each other: they do not both have to be applied within the same table.

If there is no cell spacing or cell padding in a table that contains a lot of content, particularly text, it can look as though the content of one cell is running into the content of another. This can be especially apparent if there is no border applied to the table.

If you have colored cells within a table and you want them to connect seamlessly with adjoining cells then do not include a cell spacing value. If you do, there will be a gap between the cells and the colors will not meet. To add color to a cell, insert the following piece of code: <td bgcolor= "#006666"> content</td>

Cell spacing and cell padding

Two more formatting devices for tables are cell spacing and cell padding. Cell spacing determines the distance between each cell in the table and cell padding determines the amount of space between the cell border and the content within the cells. Both of these attributes apply to all of the cells within a table. They are useful devices for ensuring that content within a table does not appear too cramped. The code for a table with cell spacing and cell padding applied to it would look like this (in this example the cell spacing is set at 4 and the cell padding is set at 6):

```
<table width="500" border="1" cellspacing="4"
cellpadding="6" bordercolor="CC9900"
bgcolor="FFFFCC">
  <tr>
    <td><p align="center"><b>One</b></td>
    <td><p align="center"><b>Two</b></td>
    <td><p align="center"><b>Three</b></td>
    <td><p align="center"><b>Four</b></td>
  </tr>
  <tr>
    <td colspan="2" valign="top">
      <p align="center"><b>Five</b></td>
    <td colspan="2" valign="top">
      <p align="center"><b>Six</b></td>
  </tr>
</table>
```

When viewed in a browser the tables will appear like this:

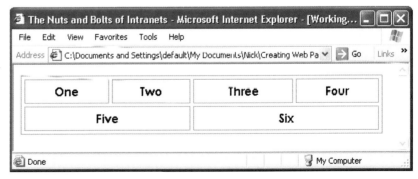

Frames

Web designers are constantly looking for ways to improve the layout and navigation of Web pages. One of the first breakthrough devices in respect of this was the innovation of frames. This is a device that displays two, or more, individual Web pages simultaneously on the same screen. This is known as a frameset, which is made up of the individual files and an additional file that determines how the files within the frameset are displayed on the screen.

The structure of a basic frameset is as follows:

Frameset container (a single HTML file that contains no content, just instructions for displaying the frame files)

```
<frameset cols="218, 786" rows="493*">
    <frame src="index.htm" name="main">
    <frame src="content.htm">
</frameset>

<noframes><body>

</body></noframes>
```

Individual frame files

Each file within a frameset can operate independently from the others and if hyperlinks are activated they can be set to open in a specific window, so that the other files remain visible on screen. One of the most popular applications for frames is for the inclusion of indexes or banner advertisements on Web pages: the main content of the page can alter while the index or banner advertisement (which is contained in a separate frame) still remain visible:

When links are activated within frames, they can be targeted to open in different locations. This can be a bit confusing for new Web designers and it is another reason why frames are best used when the designer has a reasonable general knowledge of HTML. See the next page for details of targeting links in frames.

Index   Main content

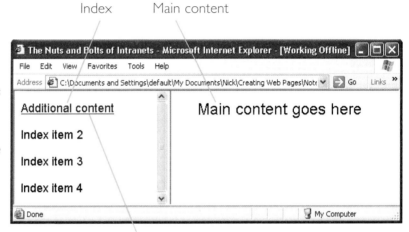

Click here to change
the main content file

Even when the main content changes,
the index remains the same

Although frames are an effective way to display banner advertisements, the latter is decreasing in popularity on Web pages since they tend to only annoy users rather than achieve their aim of selling goods and services

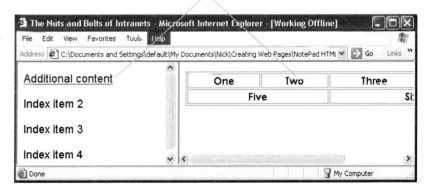

If you try and view the source code of a frame via the browser View>Source command, you will only see the code for the frameset. To view the code for individual frames, right-click (Windows) or Ctrl+click (Mac) within the frame and select View Source from the menu.

The target options that can be used when using hyperlinks within a frameset are:

- Self, which opens the linked file in the same frame
- Parent, which opens the linked file in the whole frameset window
- Top, which opens the linked file in a window outside the current frameset
- Blank, which opens the linked file in a separate window

It is also possible to target specific frames by naming them and then selecting this name as the target. See page 62 for details of this.

Links in frames

When hyperlinks are activated within a frameset there are a number of options for how the linked page appears. It can appear in the same frame as the hyperlink; it can appear in another frame of the frameset; it can appear in the whole window of the frameset; or it can appear in a completely new window. This is known as setting the target and this should be done for all links within a frameset. The following code would create a link that opens in the same frame:

```
<body bgcolor="FFFFFF">
<p><font face="arial" size="4">
<a href="image.htm" target="_self">Index Item1
</a></font></p>
```

When the link is activated, the new page opens in the same frame. This is a new file that is displayed within the existing frameset structure

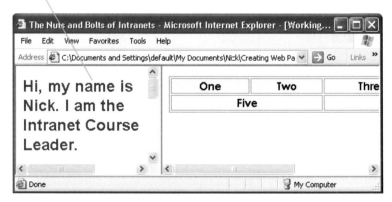

The following code would create a link that opens in the whole frameset window:

```
<body bgcolor="FFFFFF">

<p><font face="arial" size="4">

<a href="image.htm" target="_top">Index Item1
</a></font></p>
```

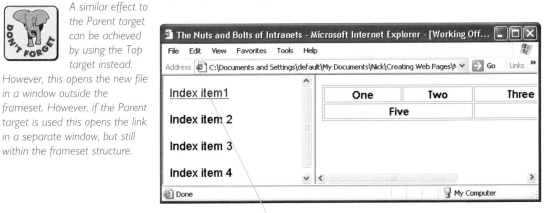

A similar effect to the Parent target can be achieved by using the Top target instead. However, this opens the new file in a window outside the frameset. However, if the Parent target is used this opens the link in a separate window, but still within the frameset structure.

A similar effect to the Parent target can also be achieved with the Blank target. However, the difference with this is that it opens the linked file in a new window while leaving the original window still available. This can be a useful way to display details such as sidebar information, while still having the original page visible.

When the link is activated, the new page opens in the whole frameset window

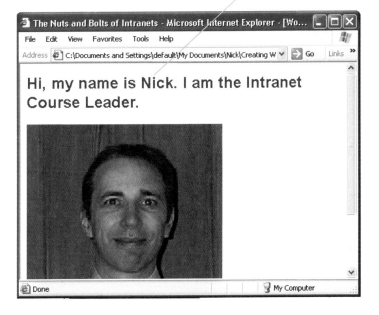

Linking to named frames

An effective use of frames is to create an index page and use this to display details in the main frame, while the index remains in view. To do this, the links in the index have to open up in another frame within the frameset. This is done by assigning a name to the main frame and then setting the target link in the index to this frame. The code for naming the frame would look like this:

```
<frameset cols="218, 786" rows="493*">

  <frame src="index.htm" name="index">

  <frame src="table_formatted.htm" name=
"main_content">

</frameset>
```

The code for targeting a link from one frame to the named frame would look like this:

```
<body bgcolor="FFFFFF">

<p><font face="arial" size="4">

<a href="image.htm" target="main_content">Index
Item1</a></font></p>
```

When the frameset is displayed and the link activated, it will appear like this in the browser:

Click here to activate a hyperlink in the index

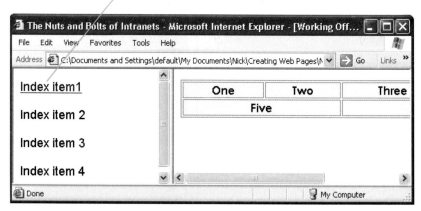

A similar effect to the one on this page can be achieved by creating a navigation bar in a table and then copying it on to all of the pages within a site. This can also be done by creating a document with the navigation table in place and then using Save As to create the subsequent files.

The linked file will open in the named frame and the index frame will remain visible:

The <noframes> tag

Some older browsers, such as Internet Explorer 3 and below and Netscape 3 and below, sometimes have a problem with displaying frames properly. Because of this there is a <noframes> tag that alerts the user to the fact that their browser cannot support frames. This is inserted at the end of the closing frameset tag and text can be added as an explanation to the user. The code for this would look like this:

```
<noframes>This is a frames site and unfortunately
your browser does not support frames. To view the
site, try upgrading your browser</noframes>
```

Although this is an increasingly less common problem due to the fact that a lot of users have more up-to-date browsers it is still worth including the <noframes> tag and text. Also, depending on the importance of the information, it could be worth including a non-frames version of the site, as an alternative to the frames one.

Sizing frames

Frames within a frameset can be set to appear at a specific size, as a proportion of the overall frameset. For instance, if you have two frames within a frameset you may want one (the index, for example) to take up 20% of the screen and the other (where the main content appears) to take up 80%. The code for creating frames at specific sizes would look like this (in this example, the frames are set to appear at 40% and 60% respectively):

```
<frameset cols="40%,60%" rows="493*">

  <frame src="index.htm" name="index">

  <frame src="table_formatted.htm" name=
"main_content">

</frameset>
```

When viewed in a browser the frameset will appear like this:

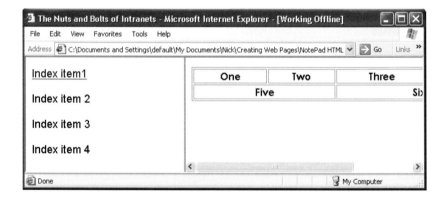

HTML editors

HTML editors offer a versatile compromise between raw HTML code and the more powerful, professional Web authoring programs. This chapter looks at how HTML editors work and shows how some of the standard Web authoring functions can be performed.

Covers

Chapter Four

About HTML editors

Once the basics of HTML have been mastered it is possible to look into some of the options for programs for creating Web pages. The most basic level is a text editor, such as Notepad, where the HTML code can be created manually.

The next step up from text editors are programs called HTML editors. These still involve creating the raw HTML code on the page but there are numerous functions and commands for assisting the process. Basically, HTML editors provide a means to insert a lot of the HTML code, leaving the designer more time to create the content of the pages.

Most HTML editors are free and can be downloaded from the Web from sites such as CNET at www.cnet.com/ Three programs to look at are:

*   CoffeeCup at www.coffeecup.com

*   NoteTab HTML at www.notetab.com

*   CuteHTML at www.cuteftp.com

HTML editors are a good option as they help you to learn how HTML works but they make it a lot easier to insert the actual coding. This lessens the chance of mistakes due to typos and forgotten tags.

Some HTML editors on CNET are demo versions of a program. If you want the full version, you have to pay for it. Other programs are shareware, which means the authors would like you to pay a nominal fee for using the software, but it is not obligatory.

HTML editors provide an authoring environment for creating HTML code and also a variety of buttons and icons to assist in the process by pre-inserting elements of the code

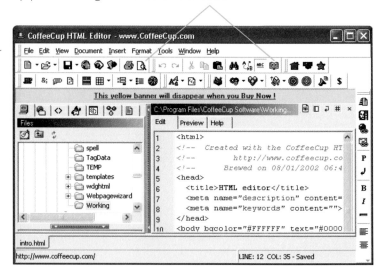

The editing environment

The rest of this chapter contains examples of some of the functions of HTML editors. They will be created using CoffeeCup, which is the most frequently downloaded editor on the Web. It contains a number of powerful editing features, while displaying a clean user interface. In general, the majority of HTML editors operate in a similar way to the following examples.

A lot of HTML editors have at least two views: the HTML code view and the preview view, where the page can be viewed as it will appear in a browser:

The available HTML tags are displayed here and can be inserted into the authoring environment by double-clicking on them

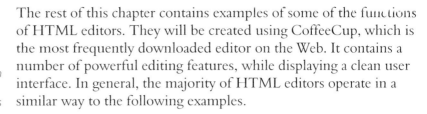

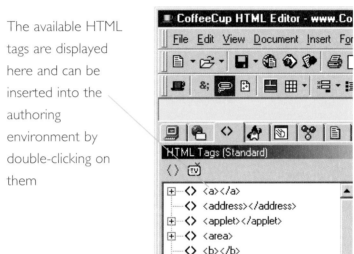

Click on the Preview tab to see how the page will be displayed in a browser and how the authoring process is progressing

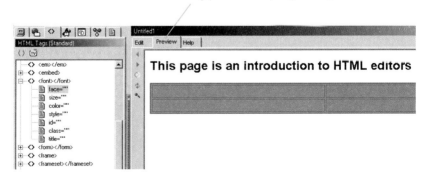

Creating pages

A good HTML editor will have a collection of templates that can be used to set some formatting parameters when a document is first opened.

Templates

1 Select File>New from Template from the menu bar

2 In the New/ Open dialog box, select a template to use and select Open

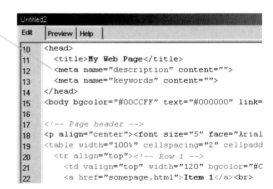

Some HTML editors' templates will insert comments about the templates. These are contained within notation that looks like this:
<!-- Add Comments here -->
and are not displayed in the published document.
Comments usually appear in a different color to the rest of the HTML code and they can be deleted if they are no use to you.

3 The code for the template is inserted into the authoring environment. This can then be edited to suit your own requirements

```
Untitled2
Edit    Preview  Help
10  <head>
11    <title>My Web Page</title>
12    <meta name="description" content="">
13    <meta name="keywords" content="">
14  </head>
15  <body bgcolor="#00CCFF" text="#000000" link=
16
17  <!-- Page header -->
18  <p align="center"><font size="5" face="Arial
19  <table width="100%" cellspacing="2" cellpadd
20    <tr align="top"><!-- Row 1 -->
21      <td valign="top" width="120" bgcolor="#C
22      <a href="somepage.html">Item 1</a><br>
```

4 Preview the code to see the framework that has been created by the template

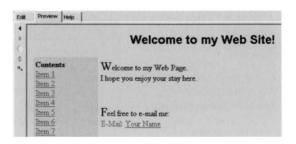

Wizards

1 Select File>New from menu bar

2 In the New/
Open dialog
box, select a
Wizard icon
and select
Open

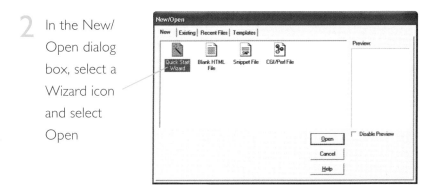

Wizards and templates only give a helping hand in creating Web pages by creating the code for various page attributes. Once this has been done the rest of the page content is up to the Web designer.

3 Enter the formatting options that will be applied to the file
created by the wizard. Click OK (or equivalent)

One common option in wizards is for creating a color scheme for all of the elements on a page, such as background color, text color and link color. This can be a useful option, but be careful with the background colors as these can get a bit tiring after a while. It is always possible to change any colors by editing the HTML code.

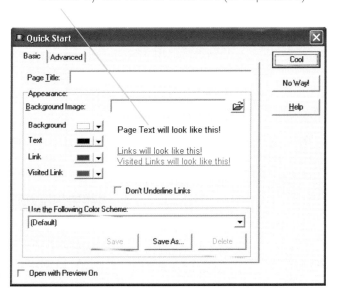

4 The formatting options are inserted into the authoring
environment. Content that is added will take on these attributes.
At this point there will be no actual content to preview

Text

Adding text is one of the fundamentals of a Web page and HTML editors handle it with ease:

1 Click here to access the HTML tags

 Some HTML editors have a text wizard where all of the text formatting options can be selected. When this is Ok'd, all of the required HTML code is automatically inserted in the authoring environment. In CoffeeCup, this function can be accessed by selecting Format>Fonts>Font Wizard.

2 Double-click on the font tag to add it to the page

3 Add any formatting tags that are required and enter the required values i.e. font face, size, color etc. Add the required text in between the tags that are inserted

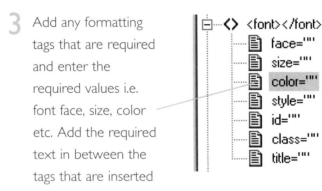

 When adding formatting for text make sure it is all contained within the <font> tag.

 Text can also be formatted once it has been added in the authoring environment. To do this, highlight the text by double-clicking on it and then select the required tag or access formatting options from the menu bar.

4 Preview the result to make sure it appears as intended

Images

Images can be added in the same way as shown on the previous page for adding text: select the required tag (in this case the <img src=" "> tag) and then enter the file name of the image to be inserted. Additional tags can then be selected to format the appearance of the image. However, most HTML editors have a function which allows you to insert and format images by selecting them from your own folders:

Always save a HTML document before any images are inserted. This will ensure that the images have a fixed point as a reference for their own tag.

1 Select Insert>Image from the menu bar

2 Browse your folders and click on an image to select it

If possible, resize images in an image editing program before they are inserted into Web pages. If images are resized in the HTML authoring software they can suffer a greater deterioration of quality.

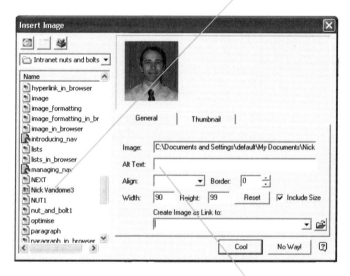

3 Enter formatting options such as an ALT tag, alignment and the desired size of the image. Select OK (or equivalent)

4 Preview the result to make sure it appears as intended

Headings

Text can quickly be converted into headings through the use of the <h> tags:

1 Click here to access the HTML tags

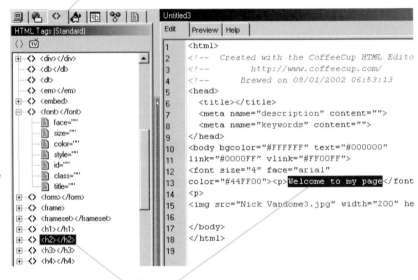

HTML headings come in six sizes: <h1> creates the largest heading and <h6> creates the smallest one.

Use a structured system of headings within a website to create a consistent look and style for the site. Make sure that you keep the same formatting for heading styles throughout a site.

2 Select an item of text and double-click on an <h> tag to add it to the text. The text is then surrounded by the opening and closing tags. Add any other headings, as required, in the same way

3 Preview the result to make sure it appears as intended

Lists

If a HTML editor has a dialog box for creating lists, this can speed up a process that can require a reasonable amount of HTML code:

1. Click on the List button on the toolbar

2. Select whether the list is to be bulleted (unordered) or numbered (ordered)

Lists can also be created in HTML editors by selecting the <ul> (unordered list) or <ol> (ordered list) tags from the tag selector panel. Individual items in the list can then be enclosed by the <li> </li> tags.

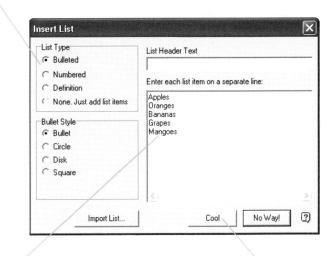

The text in a list can be formatted using the <font> and related tags, once the list has been created in the list dialog box.

3. Enter the items that are going to appear in the list. Select OK (or the equivalent)

4. Preview the result to make sure it appears as intended

Hyperlinks

Most HTML editors have the means to create all of the commonly used types of hyperlinks. If you come across one that does not offer this facility, look for another one.

Adding a standard link

In a lot of HTML editors the Insert menu enables you to insert a variety of items onto a page, such as images, sounds, horizontal rules and Flash animations.

Standard hyperlinks can be added by selecting the required tags from the tag selector, or by using a dialog box that is accessed from a toolbar or the menu bar:

1 Select Insert>Link from the menu bar (some HTML editors have this as a button on the toolbar)

2 Enter the text that will serve as the link

Text can be highlighted by double-clicking on it in the authoring environment, before the link dialog box is accessed. If this is done, the highlighted text is automatically inserted as the text that will be made into the link.

3 Type in the file to which you want the link to lead, or click here to browse your file structure and select the required file

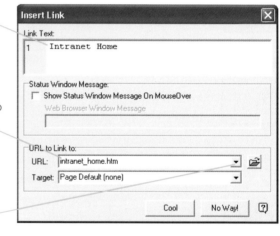

To turn an image into a link, insert it into the authoring area of the editor. Then highlight everything within the <img src> tag and then add the link in the same way as for a piece of text.

4 Preview the link to make sure it works – a pointing hand should appear when the cursor passes over it

Email links

Links to an email address can be inserted in a similar way to links to other HTML pages:

Test all email links in a browser and then send an email to make sure that you have entered the correct email address. If the address is a return one to yourself you should still test the email link. It's better that you find out any faults with the link, rather than the users.

Graphics can be used as email links as well as text. Insert the graphic into the HTML authoring area and then highlight everything in the <img src=> tag and continue in the same way as making a textual email link.

When an email link is activated on a Web page in a browser, the user's email client (such as Outlook or Eudora) opens automatically, with the recipient's email address pre-inserted in the To field.

1 Select Insert>Email Link from the menu bar (some HTML editors have this as a button on the toolbar)

2 Enter the text that will serve as the link

3 Type in the email address to which you want the email link to lead. Select OK (or equivalent)

```
<p<font size="3" face="arial"><a
href="mailto:nickvandome@hotmail.com">
Email me with your comments</a>
```

4 Check the HTML code and then preview the link to make sure it works properly

Tables

Tables are the most versatile device for formatting content on a HTML page and there a number of ways that they can be created in HTML editors:

Inserting table tags manually

When adding table tags there are a number of related items that can be inserted within these tags. These include alignment, cell padding and background color. A lot of these commands can be added to the overall table, or individual cells within it. These formatting options should be included within the table tags themselves e.g. <table bgcolor=#33CCFF>

1 Select the
<table></table>,
<tr></tr> and
<td></td> tags from
the tag selector

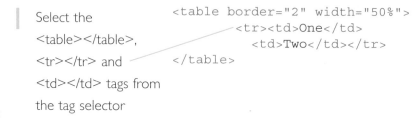

```
<table border="2" width="50%">
    <tr><td>One</td>
        <td>Two</td></tr>
</table>
```

2 Preview the
result to
make sure
it appears as
intended

Using menus or toolbars

A lot of HTML editors have wizards for creating tables that can be accessed through either the menu bar or a toolbar:

Some editors have a function for adding tables by selecting the number of rows and columns from a grid. The table is then created using these properties. Once a table has been created in this way, it can still be edited in the authoring environment.

1 Select
Insert>Table
Wizard from
the menu
bar or click
on the Table
button on
the toolbar

2 Enter the parameters for the table, such as number of rows and columns, cell spacing and cell padding, border width and table width and height. Select OK (or equivalent)

If the width of a table is specified as a percentage value then the whole table will appear in a browser window at this proportion, regardless of the size of the window. However, the formatting of the content in the table could be altered to accommodate the resizing of the table.

However, if the width is specified as a pixel value then the table will remain at a fixed size in a browser, regardless of the size of the browser window. This could mean that the user will have to scroll around the page to see all of the content.

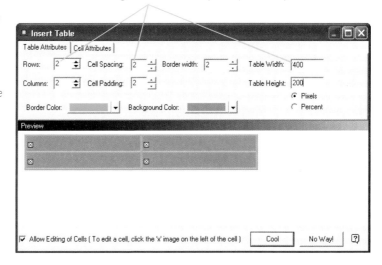

3 All of the code for the creation of the table is inserted into the authoring environment

```
<table width="400" height="200">
bgcolor="FF9900" cellspacing="2"
    <tr><!--Row 1 -->
        <td> </td>
        <td> </td>
    </tr>
    <tr><!--Row 2 -->
        <td> </td>
        <td> </td>
    </tr>
</table>
```

The format and appearance of a table can be edited in the authoring environment after the table has been inserted using the Table Wizard. Experiment with changing the parameters of the table to see how this alters its appearance.

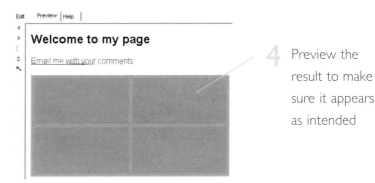

Welcome to my page

Email me with your comments

4 Preview the result to make sure it appears as intended

Frames

Frames are a HTML device that allows a Web designer to display two or more individual pages at the same time. The way that these pages appear is determined by another file that contains information about how each of the individual pages are to be displayed. This command file is known as a frameset and only contains details about the individual files. The individual files are known as frames when they are displayed with the frameset.

When creating frames and framesets, HTML editors provide a dialog box for the general format. However, some manual coding is usually still required:

Frames are one of the more complicated aspects of Web design and it is best to wait until you feel confident with HTML in general before you start working with frames.

1 Create two or more files that are going to be displayed within the frameset

3 Click on the Frames button on the toolbar

The frames dialog box can usually also be accessed from the menu bar in a lot of HTML editors.

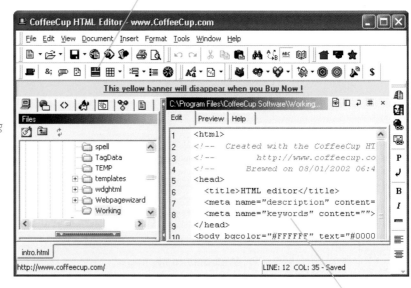

2 In the authoring environment for a new file, insert the cursor in the head part of the HTML code, not the body part. It does not matter too much where the insertion point is

4 Select the type of frameset that you want to create e.g. Two Frame, Three Frame, etc.

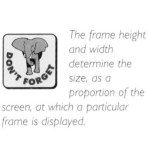

The frame height and width determine the size, as a proportion of the screen, at which a particular frame is displayed.

If the Frame Scrolling option is set to Auto, this means that scrollbars will automatically be inserted into a frame if its content extends beyond the visible screen area. If the Frame Scrolling option is set to No, then there will be no scrollbars, even if the content extends beyond the visible screen area.

All frames should be given a unique name to identify them by. This is particularly important for when it comes to inserting hyperlinks within frames and targeting where they are to open.

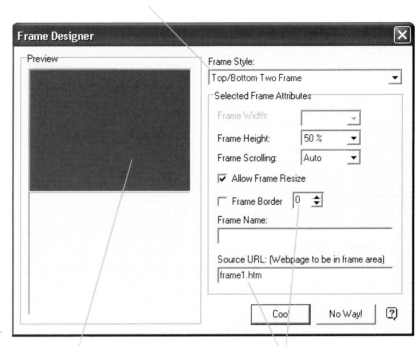

5 The format of the frameset is displayed in the Preview box. Click on one of the frames to select it

6 Enter the formatting options for the selected frame, including the file that is to be displayed in this portion of the frameset

When adding a file name for a particular frame, make sure you use the correct file extension. Some editors default to ".htm" while others use ".html". If the correct extension is not used then the frameset will not be able to display the intended files.

In the CoffeeCup HTML editor, a comment is added to the HTML code reminding you of where the code for the frameset should be placed. This is a non-printing item that does not appear in the published document.

Some older browsers have problems displaying frames but this is becoming less of an issue than it once was. If you are concerned about this, add some text in the body of the frameset file alerting users to the fact that frames are being used and, if possible, redirecting them to another page. The user will see this warning message if their browser cannot display frames.

7 Select the other frames within the frameset and enter the formatting options for them and the required file to be

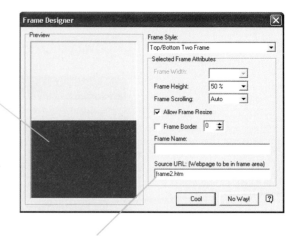

displayed in this part of the frameset. When all of the required frames have been formatted, select OK (or equivalent)

8 In the authoring environment, the code for the frameset is displayed in the head of the document. Save this file and give it a name that identifies it as a frameset file e.g. frameset1.htm

```
<frameset rows="50%,*" border="0">
  <frame name=""src="frame1.htm" marginwidth="10"
  marginheight="10"scrolling="auto"frameborder="0">
  <frame name=""src="frame2.htm" marginwidth="10"
  marginheight="10"scrolling="auto"frameborder="0">
</frameset>
```

9 Preview the result to make sure it appears as intended

Targeting links

Once a frameset has been created the issue of hyperlinks becomes important. This is because it has to be specified where a link in one frame opens in respect of the rest of the frameset. For instance, in a two frame frameset, a hyperlink can open in its own window, or the other window of the frameset, or the whole window, or a new window altogether. How hyperlinks behave in a frameset is known as targeting links:

Targeting hyperlinks in frames can be a complicated area and it takes a reasonable amount of trial and error to get it working properly, particularly if there are several frames within a frameset.

1 Open one of the files that is contained within the frameset (not the frameset file itself)

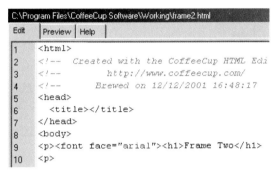

```
C:\Program Files\CoffeeCup Software\Working\frame2.html
Edit    Preview   Help
1    <html>
2    <!--   Created with the CoffeeCup HTML Edi
3    <!--          http://www.coffeecup.com/
4    <!--          Brewed on 12/12/2001 16:48:17
5    <head>
6      <title></title>
7    </head>
8    <body>
9    <p><font face="arial"><h1>Frame Two</h1>
10   <p>
```

```
<Name="Two">
<head>
     <title></title>
</head>
<body>
<p><font face="arial"<h1>Frame Two</h1>
<p><a href="frame1.html" target="Two">Link to
Frame1</a>
```

When entering a frame name as a target, make sure that it is spelled accurately. When viewed in some browsers this information is case sensitive.

2 Create a hyperlink and add a target to a named frame here. Save the file and open the frameset in Preview mode

3 When the hyperlink is activated it should open in the targeted frame

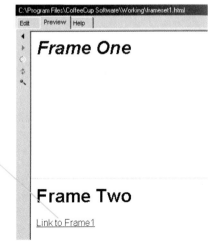

C:\Program Files\CoffeeCup Software\Working\frameset1.html
Edit   Preview   Help

Frame One

Frame Two

Link to Frame1

Multimedia

HTML editors allow designers to add most types of multimedia, such as sound, video or animated content in the form of Flash movies. Most of these items can be inserted by using the Insert menu and then selecting the required element:

1. Select Insert from the menu bar and then the item you want to insert

Multimedia elements such as sound and video files can be inserted in a similar way to inserting an image file. However, make sure that the multimedia file has the correct file extension.

2. Enter the required details in the relevant dialog box and then select OK (or equivalent)

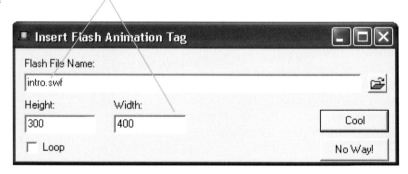

A lot of multimedia content can only be previewed when the page is viewed through a browser. For items such as Flash movies, the required plugin also has to be present.

3. The code for the multimedia element is inserted within the authoring environment:

```
<OBJECT classid="clsid:D27CDB6E-AE6D-11cf-96B8-
444553540000" codebase="http://
active.macromedia.com/flash2/cabs/
swflash.cab#version=4,0,0,0" ID=Untitled WIDTH=400
HEIGHT=300>
<PARAM NAME=movie VALUE="INTRO.SWF">
<PARAM NAME=quality VALUE=high>
<PARAM NAME=loop VALUE=false>
<EMBED src="INTRO.SWF" loop=false quality=high
WIDTH=400 HEIGHT=300 TYPE="application/x-
shockwave-flash"
PLUGINSPAGE="http://www.macromedia.com/shockwave/
P1_Prod_Version=ShockwaveFlash">
</EMBED></OBJECT>
```

Yahoo GeoCities

Online Web publishing is a cheap and effective way to achieve a presence on the Web, without the need for extensive HTML authoring knowledge or Web authoring software. This chapter explains how online publishing works and looks at one of the most popular online Web publishing sites, Yahoo GeoCities. In a step-by-step process, it details how to create an effective and functional website.

Covers

Chapter Five

How online Web publishing works

With an online publishing service it is possible to create and publish a single-page website within 10–15 minutes. However, it is also possible to create your own pages and upload them to your Yahoo GeoCities site.

Online Web publishing allows people to create Web pages by effectively removing the need for them to create HTML pages on their own computer and then transferring them onto a Web server to publish them. With online publishing, everything is done within the one website: page creation and site publishing. There are numerous sites that offer this service and there are ones for both PC and Mac users. Some of the sites are:

- Yahoo GeoCities at www.yahoo.com

- HomePage at www.apple.com

- AOL at www.aol.com

Advantages

Particularly for someone who is a novice in the Web publishing world, there are a number of advantages about online publishing:

FTP stands for File Transfer Protocol and it is the method that is frequently used to transfer Web pages from the author's computer onto the Web server that is going to host the site. For more information on FTP see Chapter Eleven.

- Everything is done in the one place and there is no need to worry about HTML editors, image editors and FTP

- Most online publishing sites have a variety of wizards and templates to make the design process relatively painless. In some cases it is just a matter of adding textual content and the site does all of the formatting and design

- Most online publishing sites are free, although in some cases there can be a fee for premium services

Disadvantages

Despite the above benefits there are also some limitations with this type of Web publishing:

An online Web publishing site may be fine when you are just starting out in your Web authoring career. However, you may quickly find that you want a bit more power and flexibility than can be offered by the wizards and templates of an online service. Some sites address this by providing a facility for editing the raw HTML.

- Design limitations. Most wizards and templates are preset and it is difficult to change any elements you don't like

- Site size. Some online publishing sites only provide a facility for publishing a single page, which can be restrictive

- Uniformity. If your site is designed with the same basic wizards and templates as thousands of others you may eventually yearn for a bit of originality

Getting registered

One of the most popular sites for creating online Web pages is GeoCities within Yahoo. Parts of this service are free but you have to register at the beginning of the process. During the authoring process there are a number of templates and wizards that can be used to help create your Web pages.

To begin the online Web authoring process you have to register. To do this, access the Yahoo website at www.yahoo.com:

Yahoo is one of the most popular sites on the Web. It offers a variety of services and online Web publishing is just one of them.

Yahoo has a number of regional sites for locations around the world. Select the one that is nearest your own geographical location.

Click on the GeoCities link

2 Click here for the free service

3 Select the service you want to use and click on the Sign up link

You will not be able to continue the registration process if you do not accept the Terms and Conditions.

4 Click on the Sign up now link

YAHOO!   Yahoo! - Help

Welcome to Yahoo!

Sign in with your ID and password to continue.

New to Yahoo!?
Sign up now to enjoy Yahoo!

- My Yahoo!   • Yahoo! Messenger
- Yahoo! Mail   • Yahoo! Chat
- Yahoo! Auctions   • Yahoo! Games
- ... and much more!

Existing Yahoo! users
Enter your ID and password to sign in

Yahoo! ID: [   ]
Password: [   ]
☐ Remember my ID on this computer
[Sign In]
Mode: Standard | Secure

Sign-in help   Forgot your password?

Some sign in details are required and the form will not be submitted if these fields are left blank. A warning dialog box will appear if any of these have been left blank and tell you what requires to be completed. Other fields are optional. Most forms like this indicate the required and the optional fields.

YAHOO!

Sign up for your Yahoo! ID

Get a Yahoo! ID and password for free access to all personalized Yahoo! services.

Yahoo! ID: [nickvandome]
Examples: "dairyman88" or "free2rhyme"

Password: [●●●●●●●●]
Must be six characters or more

Re-type Password:

5 Enter the required sign-in details and click on Submit This Form at the bottom of the page

6 Once the registration form has been sent your details will be displayed

The registration process can seem a bit long-winded just to get to the point where you can start building your page, but this is a necessary evil for this type of site.

Registration Completed: Welcome to Yahoo! nick vandome

We've sent an email to the Alternate Email Address you provided. Please read the email and follow the instructions to fully activate your account. We also recommend that you write down your password and the information below for future reference.

Your Yahoo! ID:	**nick vandome**
Your new Yahoo! Mail address:	**nick vandome@yahoo.com**
Your Alternate Email:	**nick vandome@hotmail.com** [Edit]

Click here to review your Marketing Preferences. You can select and customize the categories of communications you receive about Yahoo! products and services, or choose to opt-out of each.

[Continue to Yahoo!]

7 Click on the Continue to Yahoo button

The advertising on the Yahoo GeoCities sites is what enables the service to remain free. It is relatively unobtrusive and, since it is linked to the subject matter of your page, it does not look too incongruous.

Welcome, nickvandome

geocities.com/nickvandome

Sign up now for a premium package and your set up fee is WAIVED!

GeoCities Free

Choose a topic to determine the type of ads that will appear on your site. (Can be changed later.) If you do not want ads on your web site, please check out our **premium packages**.

○ Alternative Lifestyle	○ Friends	○ Religion & Beliefs
○ Arts & Literature	○ Games	○ Romance
○ Autos	◉ Health	○ Schools & Education
○ Business & Finance	○ Hobbies & Crafts	○ Science
○ Celebrities	○ Home	○ Seniors
○ Computers & Internet	○ Issues & Causes	○ Sports
○ Family	○ Military	○ Teens
○ Fashion & Beauty	○ Movies	○ Travel
○ Fitness	○ Music	○ Television
○ Food	○ Pets	○ Women

[Continue]

8 Select a topic and click on Continue – this determines the type of advertising on your site (not much in this world is really free)

Getting started

Once you have completed the registration you can start creating your website:

Welcome, nickvandome

geocities.com/nickvandome   **GeoCities Free**

Welcome to Yahoo! GeoCities

We just sent you a confirmation email explaining everything you need to know to build your very own web site. Be sure to **write down your Yahoo! ID and password** for future reference.

Your Yahoo! ID and Home Page Information	
Your Yahoo! ID is:	**nickvandome**
Your Alternate Email Address is:	**nickvandome@hotmail.com**
Your home page URL shortcut is:	**http://www.geocities.com/nickvandome**

Build your web site now!

There are a number of ways that you can build Web pages within Yahoo GeoCities. The PageWizards are the easiest as you just enter certain pieces of information and the Wizards perform all of the HTML creation and page formatting. However, this only offers limited flexibility in terms of layout and design.

1 Once registration has been completed, click on the Build your web site now! link

2 Click on the Yahoo! PageWizards link

Welcome, nickvandome   http://www.geocities.com/nickvandome

Yahoo! GeoCities

Upgrade to an Ad-free site Setup fee Waived!	**Start by searching for a domain name** >> www.⎢_____⎥ .com ▾ **Search**	

Web Site Accounts
▶ geocities.com/nickvandome
  ⎢ Add New Service ⎥

My Service
View My Site - www.geocities.com/nickvandome
Service Announcements

Getting Started
To begin creating your site, choose one of the tools to the right. If you're new to building web pages, try Yahoo! PageWizards.

Build My Web Site
Creating web pages is easy with these popular tools...

Yahoo! PageWizards - Easy!
Build a personal home page quickly with this simple, step-by-step method. Try it!

Yahoo! PageBuilder
Design and customize pages easily with this powerful and full-featured editor. Try it!

Enhance My Web Site
- **Web Site Add-Ons**
  Spice up your web pages with Headlines, Maps, Counters, Stock Quotes, Weather, and more.

Advanced Toolbox

File Manager
Subdirectories, HTML editing...

Easy Upload
Transfer files from your computer.

HTML Editor
Write, or cut & paste HTML code.

Site Statistics
Analyze your site's traffic reports.

Submitnet Special Offer
Submit your site to over
200 search engines
90 day free trial >>

Sanrio Themes - Choose Hello Kitty or Badtz-Maru templates from Sanrio.

Blue Angel   Flowers & Frills   Badtz-Maru

See more Sanrio PageWizards...

Popular Themes - These come with a variety of colors and looks.

Baby Announcement   Birthday Invitation   Personal Page   Party Invitation

The layout for the style of the website cannot be changed using the PageWizard, only the color of its elements.

3 Choose a style for your website and click on the relevant link

4 Click on the Launch Yahoo! PageWizard link. If you want, you can select one of the preset designs for the way your page will appear

Select a design whose color is appropriate to the type of site you are publishing e.g. blue for a more conservative site, or yellow for a more extravagant one.

Welcome, nickvandome   http://www.geocities.com/nickvandome

geocities.com/nickvandome   **GeoCities Free**

Home > PageWizards > Personal Page

Yahoo! Personal PageWizard

Launch Yahoo! PageWizard - **to begin building your Personal Page.**
This Yahoo! PageWizard will walk you through 6 simple steps that should take you about 5 to 10 minutes. What you have on your Personal Page is totally up to you. You can even choose one of the four designs below. With this PageWizard, you can choose to include the following information about yourself.

- your email address
- a picture
- brief descriptions about yourself, your hobbies and interests, and your family and friends
- and, a list of your favorite links and your friends' and family's web sites

Cool Blue   Neon Green   Think Pink   Mellow Yellow

Using the Wizard

In the PageWizard it is possible to use the Back button to return to any page in the Wizard. Once the page has been created it is also possible to return to the PageWizard and edit items on your page.

1 The Wizard opens in a new window. Click the Begin button to start adding information for your page

If you stop the Wizard process before it has been completed then any information that you have already added will be lost. The next time you login you will have to start the process from the beginning.

2 Select a background design. Click on Next

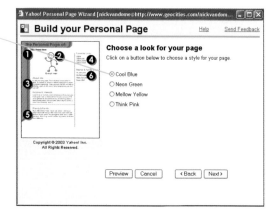

Only add your email address if you want to actively encourage feedback. Leave it blank if you do not want people to contact you. One useful method is to create an online email account (such as with Hotmail) and enter this as your email address.

3 Enter your name and email address. Click on Next

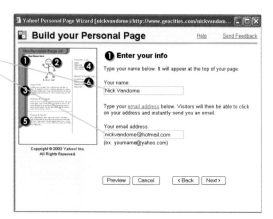

For any photographs you use on your site, make sure they are the best you can find. Your Web page will act as your window to the world so you want it to look as impressive as possible. If necessary, take some digital photographs to go on your site, or scan some hard copy pictures and use them.

Make sure you know the location on your own computer of any images that you want to use on your website.

Once images have been selected for your website, they will be displayed at a preset size. It is therefore advisable to try and create them at a relatively small size so that they do not have to be reduced too greatly when they are published.

4 To use a picture of your own for the site, check on the "Use your own image" button and click on the "Upload new image button"

5 A new window will open. Click on Browse to select a picture from your own computer

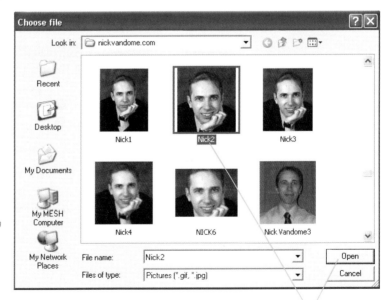

6 Select a file from your own file structure and click on Open

When the Upload button has been clicked a message will appear informing you that the picture is being uploaded and asking for your patience.

7 In the Upload Image window, click on the Upload button

When an image is uploaded, it is copied onto the Yahoo GeoCities server. This means that it can be displayed on your Web page even if your own computer is switched off or disconnected from the Internet.

8 In the "Pick your picture" window the uploaded image is displayed here. Click on Next

Think carefully about what you are going to write about yourself and your hobbies. Try to keep it brief, while making it entertaining and informative. If necessary, draft it out first so you have a chance to polish your prose.

9 Enter details about yourself and your hobbies. Click on Next

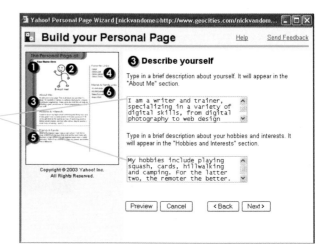

If you put links to external sites on your page, make sure they are relevant to the content of your site.

If you put links to external sites on your page, there is always the danger that users will visit these sites and then not return to your own.

You can leave all of the boxes intended for details about your family and friends blank and it is still possible to move on to the next screen.

If you do add links to websites belonging to family and friends let them know first and check that this is okay. Also, ask them if they would put a reciprocal link on their site, going to yours.

10 Enter the name and Web address for any sites you want to link to from your page. Click on Next

11 If desired, enter details about your family and friends. Click on Next

12 If desired, enter links to Web pages belonging to your family and friends. Click on Next

13 Enter a name for your page. This will appear as the page title when the page is viewed on the Web. Click on Next

Once a page has been completed and published, it is still possible to edit the content. See the next page for more details.

14 Click on this link to view the completed Web page

Yahoo GeoCities has the facility for adding items such as news headlines and weather reports to your site. For more details, see page 99.

The Personal Page of:

Nick Vandome

E-mail me!

Favorite Links:

Computer Step
Nick Vandome
Adobe
Apple

About Me:
I am a writer and trainer, specializing in a variety of digital skills, from digital photography to web design and intranets.

Hobbies & Interests:
My hobbies include playing squash, cards, hillwalking and camping. For the latter two, the remoter the better.

Editing a page

Once you have created a Web page with Yahoo GeoCities, it is possible to return to the editing environment and change certain elements of it. This is similar to creating the page with the Wizard in the first place.

Sign on to Yahoo GeoCities and click on the Yahoo PageWizards link, as shown in Step 2 on page 88

Build My Web Site

Creating web pages is easy with these popular tools...

Yahoo! PageWizards - Easy!
Build a personal home page quickly with this simple, step-by-step method. Try it!

Yahoo! PageBuilder
Design and customize pages easily with this powerful and full-featured editor. Try it!

If you want to edit a page that has been created with a PageWizard, make sure the code has not been edited manually using the File Manager function. If this has been done, the PageWizard cannot be used to edit the page. However, the File Manager option can still be used and any changes that are made will take effect on the published page.

Sanrio Themes - Choose Hello Kitty or Badtz-Maru templates from Sanrio.

Blue Angel   Flowers & Frills   Badtz-Maru

See more Sanrio PageWizards...

Popular Themes - These come with a variety of colors and looks.

Baby Announcement   Birthday Invitation   Personal Page   Party Invitation

Select the Wizard that was used to create your page initially

3 Click here and select the page that you want to edit. Click on Next

If the entire content for a particular element is removed completely, then that element will also be removed from the published page, including the section heading.

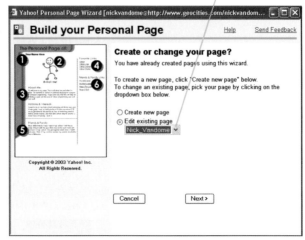

Pages in Yahoo GeoCities can be edited as frequently as you like. It is good practice to review Web pages regularly, even if you don't make any changes.

All of the elements that you do not want to be changed can be left as they are by clicking on the Next button in the relevant sections.

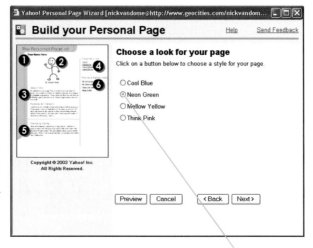

4 Edit the page element in the same way as when it was created initially. Click on Next

5 Move to the end of the Wizard and click Finish to implement the changes on your page

Using File Manager

For users who want a bit more flexibility than the PageWizards there is also an option for using the File Manager. This displays all of the items that have been created within your site and it also allows you to edit the HTML code directly. To use the File Manager:

Using File Manager to edit pages requires some knowledge of HTML code.

Log on to Yahoo GeoCities and click on the File Manager link

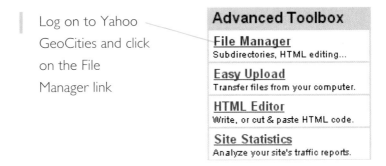

Click on the Open File Manager link

The details of your site are displayed here. To edit a page, tick this box and click on the Edit button

Click View to inspect a particular page rather than edit the code.

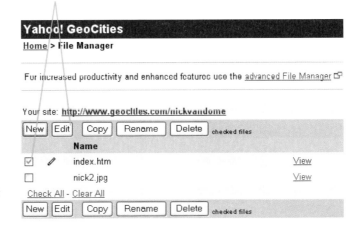

4 Make changes to the HTML code. Click on Save to save the changes that have been made

If you want to see what your editing changes look like before you save a file, click on the Preview button first and then the Save button.

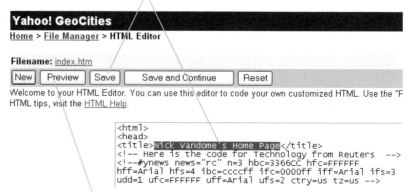

If your changes do not look as expected when you preview them, go back to the File Manager and check the HTML code. There will already be quite a lot of code in the file that is created during the creation of the page by the PageWizard. If this is altered then it could have a detrimental effect on the appearance of the page.

5 Click on Preview to view any changes that have been made

6 The changes will be made to your page as soon as you click on the Save button in File Manager

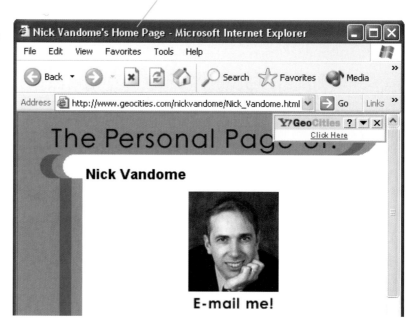

Adding elements

There are a number of website add-ons offered by Yahoo GeoCities that can be used to give an extra dimension to your site. These include news headlines, weather reports, a guestbook, an online presence that alerts people viewing your site about whether you are online or not and a countdown clock to a specific date. All of these features are added in a similar way and the following example is for adding news headlines.

These add-on features can be added to your site once the initial page or pages have been created.

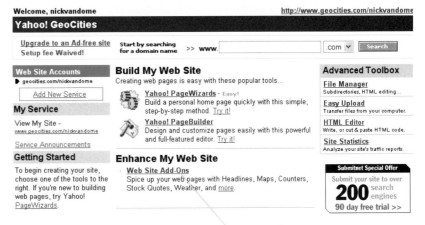

Sign on to Yahoo GeoCities and click on the Web Site Add-Ons link

The news and weather headlines are created by putting a link on your site that leads to the news or weather feed that has the full version of the item.

Click on this link to continue

Select a news feed that has something in common with the main subject of your website.

3 Select the type of news feed that you would like on your site

geocities.com/nickvandome

Home > Add Ons > News Headlines

Choose from one of the sections to find the news feed you would like.

Available Headline Sections

Headline News & Politics   **Music**
Business & Industry   **Sports**
Commentary   **Technology & S**
Community   **Canada**
Entertainment   **Latin America**
Health   **News from Asi**
Local   **News from Eur**

4 Select one, or more, news providers by checking on the boxes. Click on Next

Do not add too many news or weather feeds to your site. Otherwise these may dominate the site and your own content will be overpowered.

geocities.com/nickvandome   **GeoCities Free**

Home > Add Ons > News Headlines

Choose your headlines by checking or un-checking the boxes. Be sure to click **Next** when you're done.   Next

Available Headline Sections

☑ Technology from Reuters   ☑ MacCentral
☐ Technology from AP   ☐ ZDNet News
☐ Internet Report from Reuters   ☐ News from Space.com
☑ Tech News from CNET News.com   ☐ Science from Reuters
                                   ☐ Science from AP

5 Select a style for the headlines and the number to be displayed

Experiment with different styles of news feed to see how they look on the published page and how they appear with the rest of the content on the page.

geocities.com/nickvandome   **GeoCities Free**

Home > Add Ons > News Headlines

Choose the style and number of headlines to display in your News Headlines by checking or un-checking the boxes. Be sure to click **Generate Code** when you're done.

	Style 1	Style 2	Style 3	Number of Headlines
Technology from Reuters	○	⊙	○	3 ▾
Tech News from CNET News.com	⊙	○	○	3 ▾
MacCentral	○	○	⊙	3 ▾

After you choose a style and the number of headlines you would like, click **Generate Code**. In the last three steps you will use that code to install News Headlines to any of your web pages.

Generate Code

6 Click on Generate Code

7 Highlight this code and copy it

Step 1: Copy this code to your clipboard.

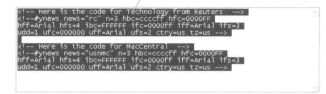

When you move to the File Manager, this will open in a new window. The original window with the step-by-step process should be kept open as you will need to return to this to complete the process.

Step 2: Click **Go To File Manager**, select the file you would like to add your News Headlines to, and paste the code in. Click **Save** and make sure to return to this page and complete **Step 3**.

[Go To File Manager]

8 Click here to go to File Manager

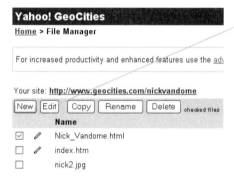

Yahoo! GeoCities

Home > File Manager

For increased productivity and enhanced features use the adv

Your site: **http://www.geocities.com/nickvandome**

[New] [Edit] [Copy] [Rename] [Delete] checked files

Name

☑ ✐ Nick_Vandome.html

☐ ✐ index.htm

☐   nick2.jpg

9 Check on the box next to the file into which you want to insert the code and select Edit

If the code is not pasted into the head section of the page then it will not work properly. It does not matter where in the head section that it is pasted.

10 Paste the code into the head section of the page. Click on Save

Welcome to your HTML Editor. You can use this editor to code your own customized HTML. Use the "Preview" button to see t on the Web. For HTML tips, visit the HTML Help

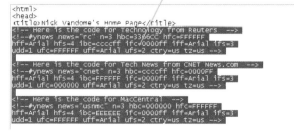

Step 2: Click **Go To File Manager**, select the file you would like to add your News Headlines to, and paste the code in. Click **Save** and make sure to return to this page and complete **Step 3**.

    Go To File Manager

Step 3: You must activate your News Headlines for them to display on your web page, click **Activate Headlines**.

    Activate Headlines

|| Return to the news headlines step-by-step page and click on the Activate Headlines button

|2 A page appears to tell you that the news headlines have been added to your page. Click on this link to view your page and see the news headlines

Welcome, nickvandome   http://www.geocities.com/nickvandome

geocities.com/nickvandome   **GeoCities Free**

Home > Add Ons > **News Headlines**

News Headlines

News Headlines have been successfully added to your page.

When news or weather headlines are added to a page the rest of the content is pushed downwards. If you decide you do not like this you can remove it by opening the File Manager and selecting to edit the required file. Then remove the code from the head section of the file, save and preview it.

|3 News headlines

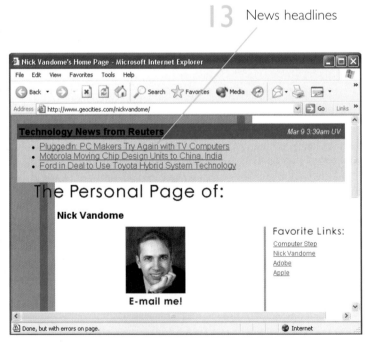

Apple HomePage

Mac users are far from neglected when it comes to online Web publishing. The .Mac website has a comprehensive range of online services, which includes a powerful online Web publishing tool, HomePage. This chapter looks at how to use the .Mac services and how to use HomePage to create effective and eye-catching online sites.

Covers

Chapter Six

Getting started with .Mac

HomePage is the Apple online Web publishing service and can be used by Mac users to create, among other things, their own online websites. HomePage is part of the .Mac online service that can be accessed at www.mac.com. There is a subscription fee for using the .Mac services.

Getting registered

To use HomePage you have to first register as a .Mac user. To do this first access the .Mac homepage at www.mac.com. Then:

You can register for .Mac directly without trying the free trial. This can be done from the .Mac homepage.

When the 60 free trial finishes, you will receive a message asking if you want to sign-up for the full service.

1 Click here to register for a free 60-day trial. The registration process is the same as for signing up for the full service

2 Enter your details as required and click on Continue to complete each page of the registration

Using iDisk

Although some functions within .Mac can be accessed via a Windows PC, the service is intended for Mac users. For instance, HomePage can only be accessed from a Mac and iDisk functions most effectively with the Mac OS X operating system.

iDisk is your own personal storage space within the .Mac service. It can be used to store files for sharing, backing up your hard disk files or store files for use in other parts of .Mac. Once you have registered for .Mac, your iDisk will be acitvated. Once this has been done, you can access your iDisk by selecting Go>iDisk>My iDisk from the Finder Menu bar in Mac OS X. As long as you are connected to the Internet, the iDisk icon will be displayed in the Finder and also on your Desktop. When you disconnect from the Internet, the icon will disappear from the Desktop, however, it will remain in the Finder. By default, items can only be added to the iDisk when you are connected to the Internet.

The iDisk icon is displayed as a separate volume in the Finder

iDisk is ideal for storing images that can then be inserted into your web pages using HomePage.

2 There are separate folders within iDisk and they are displayed here

Within iDisk there are nine folders. Three of these, Backup, Library and Software, are read-only folders for use with the .Mac service. The Public folder is for sharing files over the Internet. The remaining folders can all have files added to them from your hard drive. To do this:

The folders which can be used to store your own files are Documents, Pictures, Movies, Sites and Music. The Pictures folder is used by .Mac for items requiring images (such as iCards) and the Sites folder is used for Web pages created by HomePage.

1 Select files in the Finder and drag them over the iDisk icon and hold the mouse until the iDisk opens

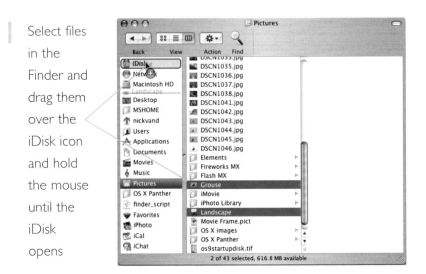

2 Hold the files over the required folder until it opens. Drop the files into the open folder

Documents can also be saved directly to the iDisk from any application by using the Save As command and then selecting the required folder within iDisk as the destination.

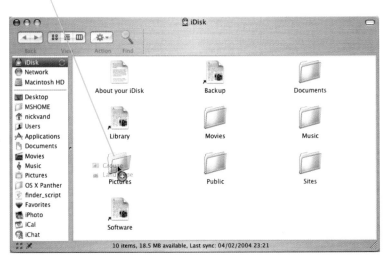

Using HomePage

Whichever .Mac service you select, you will always have to enter your membership details to log on to the site.

| Click on the HomePage button

- Mail
- @ Address Book
- Bookmarks
- HomePage

Need an Account?

Get everything you need
to extend your digital life.

(Join Now)

Sign up for a free trial

Member Name
nickvandome@mac.com

Password
••••••••|

(Enter)

Forget your password?

.mac

2 Enter your member details and click on Enter

3 Select a theme and a style for your website

Themes are preset designs that provide the foundation on which your website will be built. The themes within HomePage are more varied and diverse than some on other online Web publishing sites.

4 Click on the Edit button to edit the page and add your own content

For some theme sites there are several text boxes for adding content. This creates a newsletter format. For photograph theme sites, the emphasis is on images and the main textual content is for captioning the images.

5 To enter text, highlight the text in the text boxes and add your own words

If there are numerous text boxes on a page, make sure that they are all completed before the page is published.

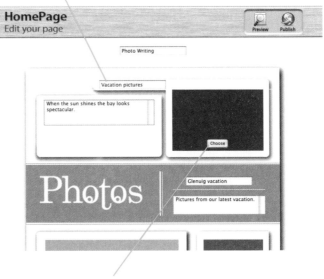

6 To add images from your iDisk, click on this button

7 Select an image that has already been added to your iDisk. Click on Choose

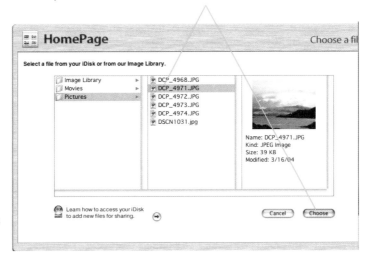

8 Once all of the content has been added, click on the Preview button to see how the final version will look

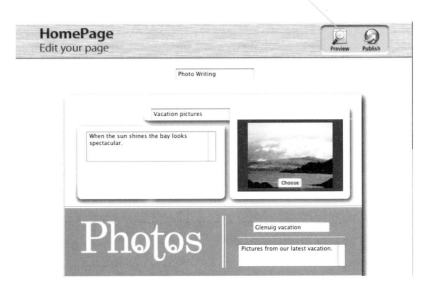

Publishing

Once you are happy with the content of your new site, HomePage can then also be used to put it on the Web for you:

Once the Publish option is selected, your page will then be live on the Web.

Click on the Publish button

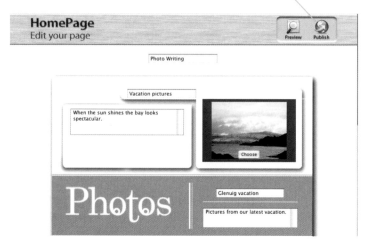

A page created and published on a Mac using HomePage can be viewed over the Web using any other operating system (such as Windows) and browser: it does not have to be viewed using a Mac.

2 A window appears telling you that your page is on the Web. Click here to view it. This is your Web page address, or URL

Try and view your published page on different computers and different Web browsers. This will give you an idea of any inconsistencies between systems.

3 Click here to send an iCard (an electronic greeting card) telling people about your page

Adding pages

Once an individual page has been created in HomePage it is then possible to add more pages to it and also create another site altogether. To add new pages to an existing site:

It is always worth adding additional pages to a site, as a single page site can become a bit monotonous for people viewing the site regularly.

1 Access HomePage within .Mac. The pages within the current site are listed here

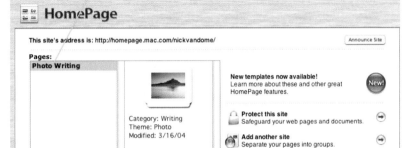

You cannot add links to other pages from within the content of an existing page. All of the links to other pages appear as textual links at the top of pages.

2 Click the Add button to add a new page (to edit the existing one, click the Edit button)

3 Select a theme and a style for the new page

It is possible to mix different themes within the same site i.e. you could have an opening page with a personal theme and then a subsequent page as a photo album.

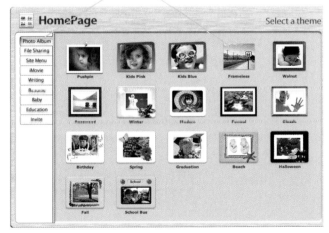

4 Click on the Edit button to add content to the new page in the same way as when creating the first page for the site

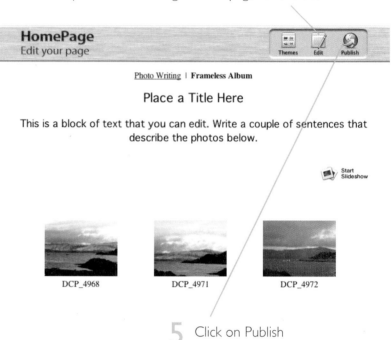

If too many pages are added to a site then the number of links that appear at the top of the site may become a bit confusing for users. Try to limit sites to approximately four or five pages.

5 Click on Publish

6 The site now comprises two pages, which can be accessed via links at the top of the page

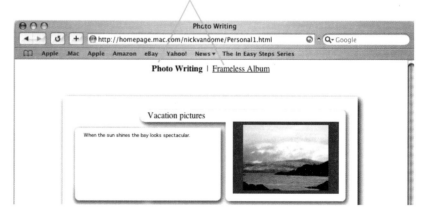

Adding new sites

As well as adding new pages to an existing site, it is also possible to create new sites within HomePage. To do this:

1   Access HomePage within .Mac. Click here to create a new site

Take a note of the full Web address (URL) of all of the sites that you create. This will help you keep track of your work and also make it easier if you want to tell people about your sites when you do not have access to a computer.

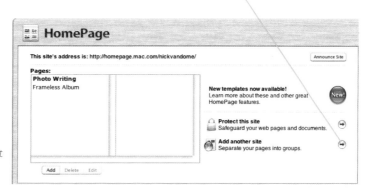

2   Enter a name for the new site and, if required, a password. Click Create Site to create the new site

There is a limit of 100 Mb on the .Mac server for each user. However, unless you are using a lot of very large images, it is unlikely that this will be exceeded by someone publishing a few websites.

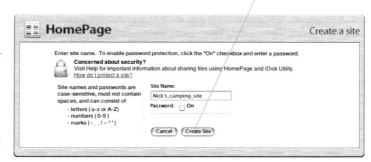

3   The new site is listed here. Click Add to add pages to the new site

4 Select a theme for the first page of the new site and create the content in the same way as described on pages 108–109

Keep all of your HomePage sites updated regularly, so that people will keep coming back to them, in the knowledge that they will be able to see new information.

5 Once the site has been created the pages within it are listed here

Make sure that different sites cover different topics. If information for separate pages is similar, then include it within the same site. There should be a clear distinction between the content of different sites, so that the user knows what they are getting when they visit a particular site.

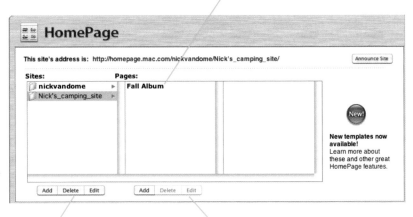

6 Click on these buttons to add, delete or edit sites

7 Click on these buttons to add, delete or edit pages within a site

Effective page design

Good websites are more than just mastering HTML and the page creation process. Thought has to be given to the overall look of a site and the elements within it. This chapter looks at some design issues connected with Web design and shows how to make pages as compelling as possible. It also covers important aspects such as updating sites and ensuring accessibility for disabled users.

Covers

Chapter Seven

Uniform style

One of the biggest failings of some websites is that they try and cram too many different styles and effects onto each page, with the end result that the site looks disjointed and inconsistent. It will probably also be difficult to navigate around. One of the reasons for this is that when a Web designer learns a new technique they are then desperate to incorporate it into their site. While a certain amount of innovation and design flair is to be welcomed, it can get out of hand and look as though it is just there for the sake of it. Two good rules to follow when creating a style for websites are:

Some design features to be particularly careful with are animated images, any kind of moving text and images that are used as background. One item to avoid altogether is text that blinks.

- Be consistent in your use of design features and overall site style

- Less is more. Sometimes the most effective designs are the ones that are simple but elegant. These can take more design skill than sites that are full of the latest design bells and whistles

Before beginning the authoring process, it is a good idea to consider some areas that contribute to an overall uniform style of a website:

Create your own hard copy style sheet and keep this handy while you are designing your sites.

- Place your navigation devices at the same location on every page. This way, the user will quickly become familiar with how to navigate around the site

- If you are using a logo, or a recurring image, keep this in the same location on every page

- Include a link back to the home page on every page of the site. This way the user will always be able to return to where they have come from and there is less chance of them feeling "lost" within the site

The type of style you choose for your site will depend to a great extent on the content of the site itself. If it is a corporate site then the style will be more formal and structured. If it is a personal site then there will be more leeway in terms of a more extroverted design. Whatever style you choose, stick to it throughout the site.

- Select two, or a maximum of three, fonts for use throughout the whole site

- Specify a font size for main headings, subheadings and body text

- Use images consistently in terms of size and positioning

Finding design ideas

Even the most inspired designers are sometimes lost for ideas and this is also true for Web designers, particularly if they have to design a lot of different sites or pages. However, there are plenty of opportunities for Web designers of all levels to stimulate their design juices. Some ways to do this include:

Use design features consistently to create an overall style for your website.

Good designers should always be on the lookout for new ideas, no matter where they occur.

- Looking at publications such as newspapers and magazines. Although there is not always a direct link between designs in hard copy publications and on the Web, they can still be a useful source for items such as use of photographs and general layout

- Advertisements. Look at billboards to see the latest techniques for text, graphics and color. Advertisement designers are usually at the cutting edge of the trade and it is a good way to see what the top professionals are up to

The effective use of color on a Web page can have a significant impact on the overall design. Try to use color as a design feature rather than just for the sake of it.

- Vary your daily routine. Take the bus to work, take a different route into town, or take up a new hobby in the evenings. Anything to shake you out of your normal routine. Although this may not have a direct impact on your Web designs, it may help you see the world a little differently and notice things that you did not before. It is surprising the amount of different things that can be incorporated into Web design

Despite the value of these processes for getting design ideas, the best way is to look at existing websites and pages to see which ones you like and why. When you are doing this, consider some of these points:

When looking at other websites be careful not to copy design ideas in full, as they may be copyrighted in some cases. Use them to get general styles and themes.

- How are images displayed?

- What is the relationship between text and images?

- What color is the page background?

- How is navigation handled?

- How much information is on a single page?

- Does the page make you want to visit it again?

Using white space

In newspaper and magazine design it has long been accepted that white space on the page is an important part of the overall design. Without it, pages can looked cramped and unappealing and it will be harder for people to read. The same is also true for Web pages and, since people find it more tiring to read text on screen, in some ways it has an even greater importance. White space can be utilized around a Web page and also within page elements themselves.

If pages are designed with white space around them, there is more chance that users with smaller monitors will be able to see the whole page on their screens.

Positioning pages

The way in which Web pages are positioned can contribute to the amount of white space that is visible when they are viewed in a browser. This is done by inserting the page content within a table and then setting the table width to less than 100% or giving it an absolute pixel width of approximately 800, or less. This will ensure that the published page takes up less than the full screen. The table can then be aligned (usually left or center) to determine where the white space appears. This is a design technique that is used by many professional designers and it is one that creates a page that is easier on the eye than those that take up the whole screen.

For more information about designing HTML tables in percent or pixels, see page 54.

Pages which contain white space around the main content are usually more effective than full screen pages

White space on a page

Since text is harder to read on screen than on paper, it is very important to add enough white space between text on a Web page.

- Insert text inside a table that only takes up part of the page

- Use a larger font size

- Insert larger spaces between lines of text

- Use plenty of headings and sub-headings

- Use bulleted and numbered lists to break up text

The difference can be dramatic.

White space should not be thought of as wasted space, but rather a deliberate and important design feature.

No white space (hard to read):

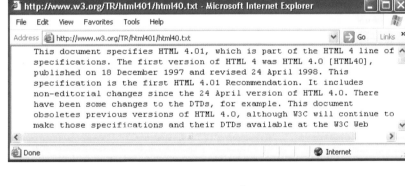

Writing for the Web is not the same as writing in hard copy. Try and be more concise on the Web and use plenty of techniques to break up the text. If you have to use a lot of text, try putting it onto several pages and using Next Page and Previous Page links to allow the user to move between them. If you are converting hard copy publications onto the Web, do not just copy it over in its entirety. Look at the text and see if it can be amended for the Web so that it is more manageable and easily digested by the user.

Plenty of white space (easy to read):

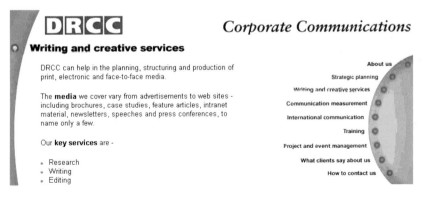

Splitting up text

Do not present large textual documents in columns in HTML. Although this can be effective in a newspaper or magazine format, it can be very annoying on a Web page: if the columns are too long the users will have to scroll to the bottom of each column and then scroll to the top of the next one to continue reading. This can be extremely annoying and will probably result in people moving on from the page fairly quickly.

As shown on the previous page, large blocks of text can be split up through the use of headings, sub-headings and bulleted or numbered lists. There are also methods for how text is displayed on the page that can make textual Web pages more appealing:

Use colored panels to present additional information

They say the Venezuelan leader is governing increasingly autocratically, that he's trying to turn this oil-rich country into another Cuba.

They also blame him for human rights abuses in breaking up the past week's protests, in which at least eight people have been killed.

The opposition's salvation is a recall referendum on the president's rule, an innovation included in the Venezuelan Constitution, backed by Mr Chavez in 1999.

TOP AMERICAS STORIES NOW
- Haiti decries Aristide 'meddling'
- Freed Guantanamo inmates go home
- Popcorn victim's $20m damages
- Four missionaries killed in Iraq

RELATED INTERNET LINKS:
- Venezuela presidency
- EU

The BBC is not responsible for the content of external internet sites

66 **The President beat them (the opposition) in democratic elections. They can't deny this reality** 99

President Chavez's supporter

- Chavez under media fire

But for the referendum to be approved, the opposition must obtain signatures from 20% of the Venezuelan electorate - some 2.4 million people.

Use tables to format text in a more digestible format. The borders can be made invisible to improve the effect

To achieve text wrap with text and images, an alignment option has to be applied to the image. To do this the following HTML code is used in relation to the image: <img src="image1.GIF" align="left">. This will then have the effect of aligning any text along the right-hand side of the image, despite the fact that the alignment option is Left. Other alignment options include: Top, Middle, Bottom and Right.

Wrap text around images, but leave enough room

Bryant blitz sends Magic crashing

Kobe Bryant's dazzling fourth-quarter display inspired the Los Angeles Lakers to a 113-110 overtime victory over Orlando Magic on Monday.

After scoring only one point in the first half, he overcame a shoulder injury to score 38 points, 24 of them in the last quarter, to steal the limelight from team-mate Shaquille O'Neal, who had 27 points and 22 rebounds.

Colors and backgrounds

The HTML code for inserting a background image appears within the <body> tag and is: <body background="NEXT.GIF">. This overwrites any background color that has been specified. The background image can then have the rest of the HTML content placed on top of it, as if it were on the bottom layer, with a sheet of glass over it.

When Web designers first discover the potential for including colors and background images on Web pages they can go a bit design crazy and create sites that look as if they have had a few pots of paint thrown at them. This is not to say that colored backgrounds and images should not be used, but if they are, they should be used sparingly and subtly. Some points to remember about colors and background images:

- White is one of the most effective backgrounds

- If you use a colored background, make sure that there is a good contrast between it and any text on top of it

- Use color as an accent feature i.e. have a white background but use colored borders or panels

- Background images can be used to good effect as watermarks e.g. they are edited in an image editor to appear very light and then inserted into the background

If small images are included as the background of a page they will be repeated to fill the page if a single image does not cover it. This is known as tiling.

If color and background images are used effectively it can have a very positive impact on a Web page:

Avoid bright or striking images as background. These can become very annoying, particularly if they are tiled to fill the page.

Colored panel

Small but effective images

White for the main background

Creating pages with Save As

At times Web authoring can be a time-consuming process, particularly if you are hand-coding HTML or using a HTML editor. Because of this, it makes sense to use as many timesaving devices as possible. The easiest of these is using the Save As command to create additional pages. Almost all programs contain this command and it is a quick and efficient way to copy pages that contain elements that appear throughout a site, such as navigation bars and tables that contain the page content. To use Save As:

Before you use the Save As command, make sure you have saved the latest changes in the current document. Otherwise, you may overwrite the original page with the one that is created with Save As.

1 Create a Web page

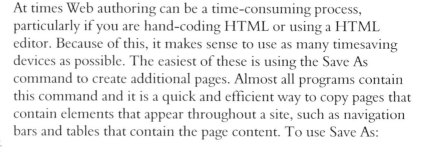

As well as giving the file created with Save As a new name, make sure that you change the page title within the <title> tag too. Otherwise it will display the same title in a browser as the original page.

2 In your HTML editor, select File>Save As

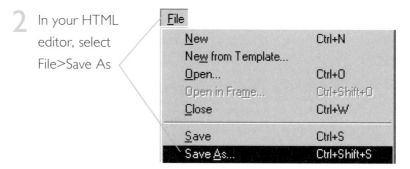

Save As is an excellent way to avoid having to rewrite a lot of the standard HTML code that appears in all HTML pages, such as the <head> and <body> tags and also any font and color information that occurs throughout all of the pages within the site.

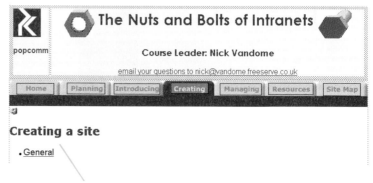

3 Remove unwanted elements and add new content

Frames and tables

Chapter Three showed how to create tables and frames in HTML and highlighted some of the advantages and disadvantages of both devices. Aside from the technical aspects of frames in relation to search engines and access technology used by disabled users, there are some design consideration to be taken into account.

Frames

Frames can be used to keep certain elements on the screen while other sections change, either by scrolling through the page or by activating a hyperlink.

Even though frames have diminished in popularity in recent years they are still used on a lot of websites and are a serious design option, particularly for items such as manuals and handbooks.

Frames can be used to reduce downloading times of complex looking sites.
Since each frame is a separate file, only one part of the frameset has to be downloaded each time a link is activated, rather than the whole page.

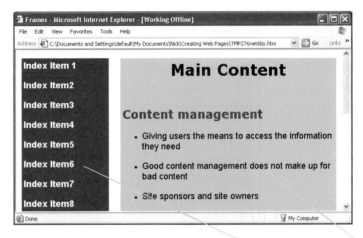

By using frames some elements remain static, even though others on the page can be altered

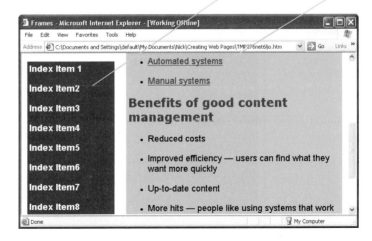

Tables

Tables can be used to create complex designs and they can also be used to create a similar effect to frames, by using them for items such as navigation bars. This design can then be replicated by using the Save As function. This can create a more streamlined design, since you do not have to worry about targeting links within a frameset, but it does mean that the table does not always remain on screen if you have to scroll down the page.

A similar effect to frames:

In most respects, tables produce a more streamlined design over frames in terms of versatility and simplicity.

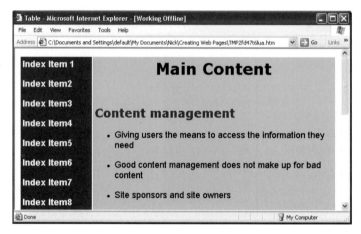

But the whole table does not remain onscreen if you move down the page:

It is perfectly possible to use tables and frames within the same Web page. However, make sure any tables fit inside the available space of the frame within the frameset.

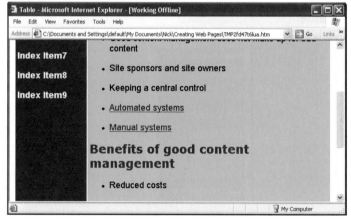

Animated effects

Vector graphics are ones where the image is based on a mathematical formula rather than actual dots of color, or pixels. Vector images can be static or they can be created with powerful animation programs such as Macromedia Flash or Adobe Live Motion.

Web pages are an ideal platform for displaying animations and animated effects, particularly with the increasing use of high speed and cable Internet connections. This has been one of the major drawbacks for animations in the past; Internet connections were just too slow to handle the amount of data needed to display some animations. However, improved connections and the development of techniques such as vector graphics and animated GIFs now mean that animation is a viable possibility for any website. But this is definitely one area where the "less is more" maxim should be applied. Just because you have the means to scatter dozens of animations around your website, it does not mean that you should. Animations should be used to attract the user and this is most effective if there are only a small number of animations. A few general rules should also be followed with animations:

- Keep them small, in both file size and onscreen size. Animations can be an effective way to display items such as logos

For an overview of animation and Flash, see Chapter Ten. There is also a book titled "Flash MX in easy steps" that takes an in-depth look at the program.

- Be very sparing with animated text. This can become irritating in the extreme if there is a lot of it

- Use animation for specific purposes, not just because you have found some nice effects on a website

Finding animations

Animated GIFs and Flash files are two of the most popular forms of animation on the Web. Flash files have to be created using the Flash program, but there are a large number of websites where animated GIFs can be downloaded and used. Some to try are:

Animated GIFs can be inserted into Web pages in the same way as static images. It is only when they are viewed through a browser that the animated effect becomes apparent.

- www.gifs.net

- www.animfactory.com

- www.animatedgif.net

Accessibility

Although it is good practice for all Web designers to make their sites as accessible as possible, it is more applicable to some types of sites than others. If you are designing your own personal site, you may not consider it to be of paramount importance. However, if you are designing a corporate website, or an ecommerce site, then you should try and meet at least some of the requirements for people using access readers.

Overview

Since the World Wide Web has evolved as an egalitarian medium of communication, intended to be used by as many people as possible, disabled users are not precluded from this online community. A number of devices are available to help people view the Web and some of these are for people who are blind or have impaired eyesight. There are varying kinds of on-screen access readers, that translate the information on a Web page and then read it to the user through a synthesized voice box. This obviously has an implication for Web designers, as they have to try and ensure that their designs are compatible with these readers. This is sometimes a considerable task, as there are a number of elements in Web design that can cause problems. Some of them are:

- The labelling of images. All images should contain an ALT textual tag so that readers can read the description of the image for those that cannot see it

- Frames. This can cause a certain amount of confusion for some access readers as they do not always know which piece of information belongs to certain frames. Recent developments in technology has enabled some readers to overcome this problem

There has already been some court activity in relation to the accessibility of websites. These have tended to focus on corporate sites but it is something that all Web designers should be aware of.

- Tables. Some access readers interpret information column by column while others read it by rows. This can have a considerable impact on the way information is laid out in a table

- Javascript. If you are using elements of programming languages such as Javascript on a Web page this could cause problems for the access reader

Try and see a Web access reader in operation, as this will give you a better understanding of the constraints under which they work.

- Navigation. Main navigation, and if possible all navigation, should be created in plain HTML, rather than using techniques such as rollovers

- Text and color contrast. Access readers can have problems interpreting text if there is not a strong enough contrast between it and the background on which it has been placed.

Checking accessibility

There are dozens of accessibility issues for Web pages and it would be unrealistic to expect all designers to strictly follow them all. There are a number of websites that provide information about checking the accessibility of your website. The one responsible for setting the standard for website accessibility is the W3C site that contains comprehensive details of accessibility issues on their website at www.W3.org/wai:

Some of the accessibility issues for Web pages are quite complex and you need a good knowledge of HTML to understand them. However, if you follow the more straightforward guidelines then this should overcome a good number of accessibility issues.

Web Accessibility Initiative (WAI)

news - about - participation - resources

"The power of the Web is in its universality. Access by everyone regardless of disability is an essential aspect."
-- Tim Berners-Lee, W3C Director and inventor of the World Wide Web

If you want to run a diagnostic test on your website, to check it for accessibility, try Bobby at www.cast.org/bobby:

Updating

Because of the nature of the medium, Web pages can be updated almost instantly when there is new information to add. Because of this, users expect websites to be current and up-to-date. One of the cardinal sins of Web page creation is to include a "last updated" date on a website that is months, or years, out of date. Even if there has been no reason to update the page in that time, users will presume it is out of date and move on to something else.

Updating is an essential part of creating Web pages: in some ways the easy part is getting the site up and running; the hard work comes when you have to try and keep it up-to-date. This should be tackled in a structured way:

Updating should be looked at as a necessity rather than a chore that can be ignored if you don't feel like it. The Web is littered with sites that are virtually redundant because they have not been updated properly.

- Look at the information on your site and identify items that require to be updated weekly, monthly or not at all

- Draw up a timetable for site housekeeping, and stick to it

- Include a "last updated" date on your site

- More importantly than above, include a "next review due" date on your site. This will show users that the site will be looked at and updated in the near future. Also, once the review date has passed, this can then be included as the last updated date

Update your Web page design as well as the content. Design trends move very quickly in the virtual world and designs can quickly begin to look tired and jaded. Consider redesigning at least every six months. This does not have to be a radical overhaul but at least a general make-over.

Including Last Updated and Next Review Date entries on your site gives users confidence that it is being updated regularly

Contacts

About Us

News

Last Updated:
08/24/04

Next Review
Date Due:
10/19/04

Navigation

Enabling users to navigate quickly and easily around a website is vital to its success. This chapter looks at some of the basics of navigation and shows some of the options and techniques that can be used to make the process as smooth as possible.

Covers

Chapter Eight

Types of hyperlinks

Hyperlinks provide the infrastructure for moving between other Web pages and sites. They can be applied to text or graphics and, within limits, can be presented in a variety of ways:

Standard links

Chapter Three showed how to create standard textual and graphical hyperlinks. Standard textual links appear in blue and are underlined. Standard graphical links are only identified as such when the cursor is placed over them in a browser and it turns into a pointing hand (unless they are created with a colored border).

Customized links

Cascading Style Sheet code can be inserted directly into HTML documents or the HTML file can be linked to a separate Cascading Style Sheet file. Cascading Style Sheets can be used to format numerous elements within HTML documents, not just hyperlinks.

Textual hyperlinks can be customized to appear in a variety of different formats, such as without the underlining. This is done through the use of Cascading Style Sheets (CSS). The following code shows how a CSS can be applied to the formatting of a textual hyperlink:

```
<style type="text/css">
<!--
p {  font-family: Arial, Helvetica,
sans-serif; font-size: 14pt; color: #006600}
a {  font-family: "Century Gothic";
font-size: 18pt; font-style: italic;
font-weight: bold; text-decoration: none}
-->
</style>
</head>
<body>
<p>CSS items automatically take on the
formatting of the specified tag</p>
<p><a href="index.htm">This includes hyperlinks</a>
</body>
```

For a more detailed look at Cascading Style Sheets, have a look at the website at www.w3c.org/ which provides the definitive information about HTML code and related items.

When viewed in a browser this hyperlink would be displayed like this:

```
The Nuts and Bolts of Intranets - Microsoft Inter...
File   Edit   View   Favorites   Tools   Help
Address  C:\Documents and Settings\default\My Docu    Go   Links

CSS items automatically take on the
formatting of the specified tag

This includes hyperlinks

                                    My Computer
```

Rollovers can be an extremely effective device for navigation buttons. Plain colored buttons are usually the most effective. Try and make sure that the transformation from one button to another is not too dramatic. Keep it to similar colors if possible, e.g. blue and light blue.

To view the HTML code of a Web page, select Edit>View Source from the browser menu bar. This will then appear in a text editor. It is then possible to copy and paste any parts of it that you want to use in your own files.

Rollovers are one item that can be difficult for access technology devices to read. If possible, contain the information in a plain HTML format too, not just in Javascript.

Rollovers

Rollover images are ones that change in appearance when the cursor is moved over them in a browser. In addition, it is also possible to insert a hyperlink into the rollover so that is can be used as a navigational device. Rollovers are created using Javascript code which is a complex computer language that requires considerable training and experience. Some professional programs such as Dreamweaver, GoLive and FrontPage have the capability to create rollovers automatically and this is a very worthwhile function. Another way to create rollovers is to look at the source code of a Web page that contains rollovers. Copy the code into a text editor or a HTML editor and try and amend it for your own requirements.

Creating HTML effects

- Slices — dividing images up into smaller segments for faster c
- Rollovers — images that change appearance when the cursor browser

When the initial image is rolled over with the cursor it changes appearance.

Creating HTML effects

- Slices — dividing images up into smaller segments for faster
- Rollovers — images that change appearance when the cursor browser

This is a rollover image

If a hyperlink has been inserted, the user can also click on it to move to another location

Navigation bars

Consistency is an important element of a website and one of the best ways to achieve this is through the use of navigation bars. These are collections of hyperlinks, or buttons, that provide the navigation for the whole site. Ideally, these navigation bars should appear on all pages within a site so that users can quickly become familiar with how to get around the site, regardless of which page they are on. Depending on the complexity of the site, several navigation bars could be used, such as those for main and secondary levels.

Navigation bars do not have to just contain navigational links. They can also contain items that are required to appear on all pages of a site, such as a logo or a search engine.

Most sites for large corporate companies contain at least two or three levels of navigation bars and this is an excellent way to create site consistency.

Corporate sites frequently have several levels of navigation bars, such as this one for Apple:

Main navigation bar   Secondary navigation bar

Navigation bars can help to create a brand image for a site, as the elements appear on all of the pages that the user sees.

Mac OS X Panther.
The evolution of the species.

With over 150 innovative new features, it's like having an all-new Mac.

Creating a simple navigation bar

It is possible to create an effective navigation bar through the use of a table and plain textual hyperlinks:

It is possible to create navigation bars, using collections of images. This can include rollover images and is usually achieved using professional Web authoring software. While this can create an impressive design, it is simpler to use the procedure on this page. See the following pages for details on producing an image-based navigation bar.

1 Create a table with one row and the required number of columns

2 Make the table borders invisible and give the table a background color

3 Add text into each cell and format each text block

| Home | Books | Travel | Hobbies | Family |

Once a navigation bar has been created in this way it can then be copied onto other pages by selecting the table and copying it. Then, open up a new page and paste in the whole table i.e. the navigation bar. Alternatively, use Save As on the original page with the navigation bar and then create a new page containing the navigation bar in this way.

4 Turn each text block into a hyperlink

| Home | Books | Travel | Hobbies | Family |

Creating an image-based navigation bar

Image-based navigation bars are achieved by creating a series of buttons that function as rollover images which include a hyperlink within them. This uses Javascript programming and unless you are proficient in this the best alternative would be to use a Web authoring program such as Dreamweaver, which is used in the following example. To create an image-based navigation bar:

When creating an image-based navigation bar create the original images for each button at exactly the same size, usually with the same text, e.g. Home. The rollover effect is achieved by altering the image color and/or text color of the image that is displayed when the cursor passes over it i.e. the rollover effect is activated.

1 In the Insert Navigation Bar dialog box, give the first element (the first button) of the navigation bar a name

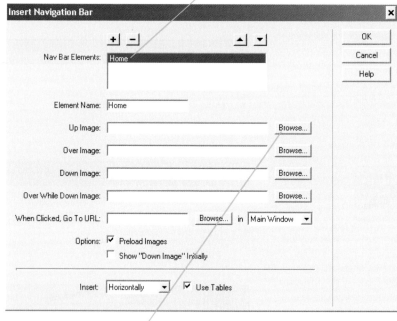

Other professional Web authoring programs, such as FrontPage and GoLive, have functions for producing navigation bars. Also, there are a number of programs that can be downloaded for free from the Web that provide the means to create rollovers and navigation bars. One site that offers access to programs of this type is CNET at: www.cnet.com/

2 Click here to browse your file structure for an image that will appear in the Up state of the button. (This is how the button will appear normally, when the cursor is not being rolled over it)

3 Add an image for the Over state of the button. This is the image that will appear when the cursor passes over the button. Make sure that it is different from the Up state in some way i.e. a different color

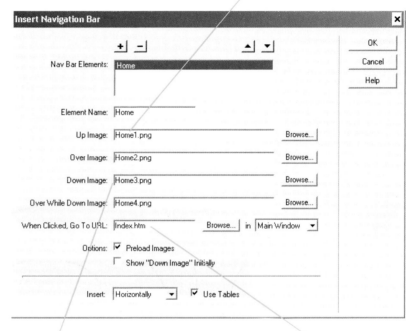

Images can also be added for the Down state, which is while a button is in the process of being pressed, and the Over While Down state which is while a button is being pressed and the cursor is then rolled away from it.

4 If required, add images for the Down and Over While Down states of the button. These are optional (see Tip)

5 Enter a URL. This will be the page that is opened once this button is clicked on by the user

There are no hard and fast rules as to where to place navigation bars, but as a general guide, place main navigation bars horizontally and secondary ones vertically. The main deciding factor will be the overall design of the website.

6 Repeat steps 1–5 for all of the elements of the navigation bar. Select if the navigation bar will be created horizontally or vertically

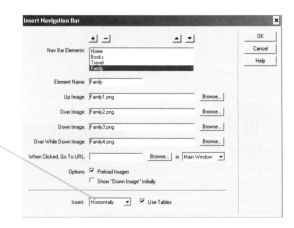

7 When the navigation bar is viewed in a browser, it will appear as a horizontal or vertical collection of button images

Navigation bars created with rollover images can cause some accessibility problems for partially sighted or disabled users who are using access technology readers to read Web pages.

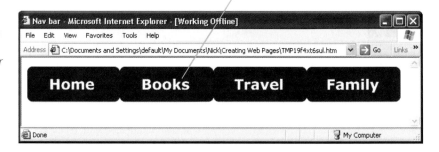

To see the code used to make up an image-based navigation bar, find a site on the Web that uses one and look at the code by selecting View> Source from the browser. This should give you some idea of the complexity that is involved in creating this type of device, and the benefit of using a professional Web authoring program.

8 When the cursor is rolled over an element of the navigation bar, the Over image is displayed and the hyperlink becomes active

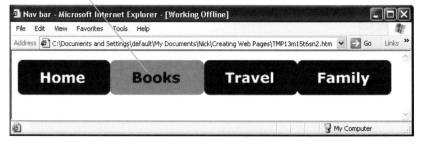

Linking to external sites

Hyperlinks to external sites, i.e. sites on the Web outside your own site, can be created in a similar way to those to other pages within your site. The important thing to remember here is that the links have to be absolute, which means they have to include the full Web address (URL) of the targeted site. To create a link to an external site the following code is created:

```
<p>Look at <a href="http://www.macromedia.com">
Macromedia</a>for Web authoring programs</p>
```

Links that go to other pages within your own site are known as relative links i.e. they are relative to the other pages within the website.

When this is viewed in a browser the link will appear in the standard format but when it is accessed the external site will open:

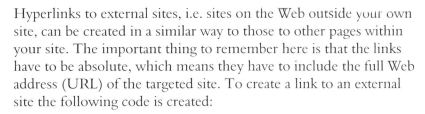

Links to external sites only work if there is an active Internet link. If you try and access an external link when there is no Internet access your computer will try and connect you to the Internet. For other users this should not be an issue since they will only be viewing your site over the Internet.

Look at Macromedia for Web authoring programs

Creating a site

If your website contains links to external sites, make sure you check regularly to make sure that these sites are still active and using the same Web addresses.

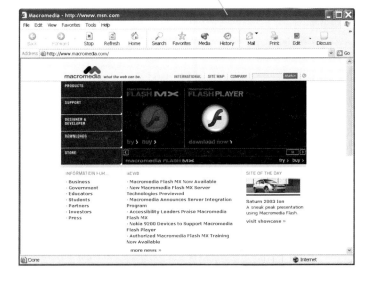

Email links

As well as linking to other Web pages, hyperlinks can also be created to access email addresses. When this is accessed it opens up the user's email program rather than another Web page. Email links can be added to either text or graphics: they can appear on the page as the email address itself or it can be a graphic or label that contains the email link in the HTML code. To create an email link the following code is used:

Email links on a website are a great way to get feedback from users. Include your own email address as the link and then ask users for comments or suggestions about the site.

```
<p align="center"><a href="mailto:nick@vandome.
freeserve.co.uk"><font face="Arial, Helvetica,
sans-serif" size="3">email your questions to
nick@vandome.freeserve.co.uk</font></a></p>
```

The Nuts and Bolts of Intranets

An effective way to display an email link is to add the link to an icon of a letter or a mail box. These can be found in a lot of clip art collections and also on the Web itself. Try typing "email icons" into a search engine to find some sites.

Course Leader: Nick Vandome

email your questions to nick@vandome.freeserve.co.uk

When this is viewed in a browser the user can click on the link, which will activate their email program, with the relevant email address pre-inserted in the To box::

Try not to include email addresses to anywhere other than your own one. This is because it is best to avoid links that take users away from your site, unless it is to send you an email. Also, other people may get a shock if they suddenly get an unexplained email.

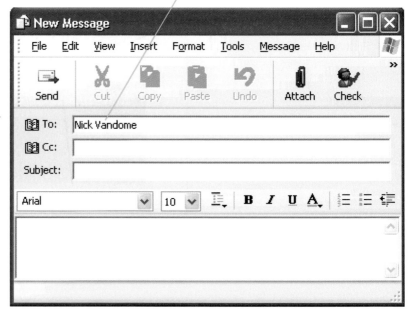

Creating image maps

Image maps are a device where one or more hyperlinks are added to an image. This then enables the user to click on various areas of an image and be taken to a different location in each case. This is done by assigning areas on the image according to specified co-ordinates that will serve as the areas for the hyperlinks. The hyperlinks are then added to these areas. They can either be rectangles, ellipses, or asymmetrical shapes that are drawn by hand.

The following code could be used to create an image map:

Image maps can be created with client-side code or server-side code. Client-side code means that the image map code is inserted directly into the HTML file. Server-side code means the code resides on the server that is hosting the page.

The most common form is client-side, like the example on this page, and this is what most people should use.

```
<p><img src="PUBLISHING_NAV.png" width="764"
height="54" usemap="#Map" border="0">

    <map name="Map">

        <area shape="rect" coords="557,7,648,27"
href="RESOURCES.htm">

        <area shape="rect" coords="448,6,540,29"
href="PUBLISHING.htm">

        <area shape="rect" coords="345,6,421,28"
href="EDITING.htm">

        <area shape="rect" coords="230,5,317,29"
href="CAPTURING.htm">

        <area shape="rect" coords="117,5,211,29"
href="EQUIPMENT.htm">

        <area shape="rect" coords="24,5,89,29"
href="INDEX.htm">

        <area shape="rect" coords="668,6,750,28"
href="SITEMAP.htm">

    </map>
```

The code for creating image maps can be a bit daunting. Professional Web authoring programs make the whole process a lot easier by allowing you to draw the area you want to make into an image map directly onto the image itself.

Image maps in action

When the image map is viewed in a browser the hyperlinks are not visible unless the cursor is passed over them. In the following example, though, the areas of the hyperlinks have been added:

Use images for image maps where it is clear as to the location of the hyperlinks within it. Actual maps are very effective in this regard as each area can be made into a hyperlink. Also, groups of people are a good option as each person can have a hyperlink attached to them that goes to a page containing their own personal information.

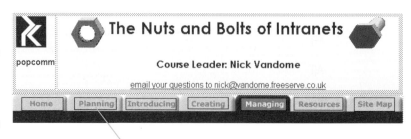

The different hyperlinks within an image map enable different pages to be accessed from a single image

Make sure that the hyperlink areas within an image map do not overlap. If they do, the user may be taken to the wrong location when they click on a particular part of the image. With some programs, it is possible to change the order in which the hyperlinks areas are stacked on the page. But in general, it is better to keep them all apart if possible.

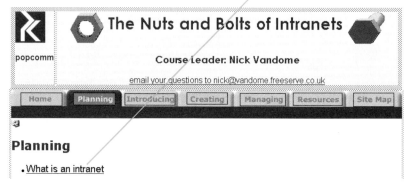

Site maps

Site maps should be updated regularly. Otherwise users will stop looking at them and lose confidence in the overall accuracy of the site. It is one of the more laborious tasks of Web design, but whenever a new section is added to a site, make sure that the site map is also updated.

A "site map" is a simple navigational device that gives the user a point where they can see all of the sections on a website, and access them through hyperlinks. In effect it is an index of all of the main areas on the site. Site maps can be created in a variety of styles and formats, but the important thing to remember is that they are readily available from anywhere on the site. This way the user is never far away from an index of the contents of the site.

Site maps can be created in a graphical format (in this case as a series of road signs)

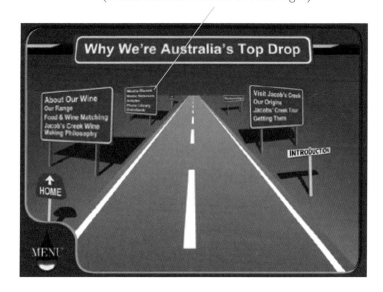

Make sure that the site map is readily accessible from all other areas of the website, through the use of a highly visible hyperlink.

If you are using a plain textual index as a site map, include an A–Z bar at the top. This should include links to all of the alphabetic sections of the site map. These links can be created to the relevant sections on the page through the use of anchors. For more on anchors, see Chapter Three.

Site Map

Or they can be created as a plain textual index

General	Creating	Introducing	Managing
Overview	HTML basics	Setting up a team	Content management
Resources	HTML advanced	Implementing	Reacting to events
	HTML tools	Winning over users	Needs commitment
	Multimedia	Quick Wins	Create updating guidelines
	PDF	Avoiding problems and pitfalls	Allowing users to create their own sites
	Image editing		
	Navigation		Publishing guidelines
	Pre-publication checks		

Three-click navigation

The key to a three-click navigation system lies in the accuracy of the site map and the level of detail that it contains. If your site has a limited number of pages (e.g. 20 or less) then it will be possible to put a link to all of them on the site map. However, if you have 100s of pages on your site you may have to decide how far into the file structure you want the site map to display i.e. the second level of the hierarchy, or the third, or so on.

The more levels that your site contains then the greater the likelihood that the user will have to use more clicks to drill their way through it. The crucial thing is how much detail you want to include on the site map.

One of the most common phrases used in relation to getting around websites is three-click navigation. This refers to the best-practice idea that you should be able to access all areas of a website within three mouse clicks, regardless of where you are on the site. This may sound like a daunting task, but it can be made very simple, through the use of a navigation bar and a site map. If a navigation bar is created that contains a link to the site map, and this bar then appears on all pages of the site, the user is always only one click away from the site map and then one more click away from the areas of the site. In a lot of cases this could even achieve a two-click navigation system rather than a three-click one:

1 Create a navigation bar that contains a link to a site map

2 Ensure the site map contains links to all of the main pages and areas within the site:

Site Map

The title "Site Map" is not the most exciting in the world. Depending on the type of site, try something a bit more welcoming such as "Getting Around" or "Find Your Way".

General

Digital photography today

Uses for digital photography

Advantages

Disadvantages

Capturing

The resolution riddle

Compression

Color depth

Photographic techniques

Images of people

Editing

Downloading

What the software does

Entry level programs

Professional programs

File formats

3 From any page on the site the site map should still be accessible with one click

Use natural borders

4 This allows you to access the site map and so the navigational process can continue onto another area of the site if required

Home	Equipment	Capturing	Editing	Publishing

Site Map

General	Capturing	Editing	Equipmeı
Digital photography today	The resolution riddle	Downloading	Cameras
	Compression	What the software does	Accessories
Uses for digital photography	Color depth	Entry level programs	Computer

Site linkage

Good site navigation is about making it as easy as possible for users to make their way around your site. Look at some websites that you find easy to navigate around and see what devices are used. Generally, if you find a certain technique useful then users of your own site will do so as well.

In addition to a site map it is also important to include general navigational devices throughout a site. These are designed to help users find their way through a site and also get back to the Home Page at any time. Two of the best devices for this are:

- Home Page button

- Next and Previous buttons

A Home Page button should appear on the navigation bar on every page of the site and it offers the user a quick option to return to the Home Page from wherever they are. Next and Previous buttons should be used when long passages of text are used and broken up on to several pages for ease of use. If this is the case, each page should contain a link to the next and/or previous page of the text:

For a corporate site, the Home Page link will frequently be the company logo. For a personal site, it could be anything from a picture of the site author to a graphic depicting their favorite hobby. Whatever is used, make sure it is small and unobtrusive as users will only want to use it when they want to move back to the Home Page.

A Home Page button link should be placed on the navigation bar to ensure that it appears on every page of the site. This can either be a graphical link or a textual one, or both

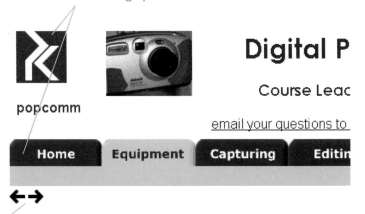

popcomm

Digital P

Course Leac

email your questions to

| Home | Equipment | Capturing | Editin |

Include Next and Previous buttons to help users navigate through long passages of text.

Entry level

- 2–3 million total pixels (megapixel)

- Good for Web images and email

- Acceptable for most printed images

Images

Most websites benefit from the inclusion of images. However, they have to be used carefully to achieve the maximum effect. This chapter looks at the types of images that should be used on Web pages, how to obtain them and how to make the most of them when they are inserted into Web pages.

Covers

Chapter Nine

Image formats for the Web

GIF comes in two varieties, 87a and 89a. These are more commonly known as nontransparent GIFs and transparent GIFs respectively. With a transparent GIF the background can be made see-through. This is very useful for Web images: if you want the subject of an image to appear against the Web page background, you can do this with a transparent GIF.

Digital images can be created and saved in a variety of different formats. This is not always immediately apparent when you view the images on screen, but the file format can have important implications as far as the use of the image is concerned.

The two main areas that designers of image file formats consider are:

- The size of files – how to get good quality images that do not take up a lot of disc space

- The quality of images – how to produce images that give the best published quality possible

Because of this, particular file formats are used for inclusion on Web pages.

GIF files

GIF (Graphical Interchange Format) is one of the two main file formats that are used for images on the Web (the other being JPEG). It was designed with this specifically in mind and its main advantage is that it creates image files that are relatively small. It achieves this principally by compressing the image by removing unnecessary or irrelevant data in the file.

There are two methods for compressing digital images; lossy and lossless. Lossy means that some image quality is sacrificed, while the lossless method only discards image information that is not needed. JPEGs use lossy compression while GIFs use lossless compression.

The main drawback with GIF files for digital images is that they can only display a maximum of 256 colors. This is considerably less than the 16 million colors that can be used in a full color image. Therefore photographs in a GIF format may lose some color definition and they will not have the same range of color subtleties as a format that can display the full range of colors.

Despite their narrow color range GIF is still a very useful and popular format. It is excellent for displaying graphics and even photographs can be of a perfectly acceptable standard for display on the Web. Add to this the fact that it can create very small image files and it is easy to see why GIF is so popular with Web designers.

JPEG files

JPEG (Joint Photographic Expert Group) is the other main file format for Web images and it is the one that, as the name suggests, specializes in photographic images. A lot of digital cameras automatically save images as JPEGs.

JPEG images only achieve their full effect on the Web if the user's monitor is set to 16 million colors (also know as 24 bit). Most modern monitors are capable of doing this but, in some cases, the user may have set the monitor to a lower specification. If you are concerned about how your images are going to be viewed it may be worth putting a note on your site suggesting that the screen be set to 16 million colors for full effect.

As with GIF, JPEG compresses the image so that the file size is smaller; it is therefore quicker to download on the Web. One downside to this is that the file is compressed each time it is opened and saved, so the image quality deteriorates correspondingly. When a file is opened it is automatically decompressed but if this is done numerous times then it can result in an inferior image.

The main advantage of JPEG files is that they can display over 16 million colors. This makes them ideal for displaying photographic images. The color quality of the image is retained and the file size is still suitably small.

PNG files

The PNG (Portable Network Group) file format is a relatively new one in the Web image display market but it has the potential to become at least as popular as GIF and JPEG. It uses 16 million colors and lossless compression, as opposed to JPEG which uses lossy compression. The result is better image quality but a slightly larger file size. Since PNG is a less common format there are a few factors to bear in mind when using it:

- Not all browsers support the PNG format. This will undoubtedly change as its use becomes more widespread but it is a consideration at the moment

Note the following graphics file extensions/ suffixes:

GIF files – .gif
JPEG files – .jpeg
PNG files – .png

- PCs and Macs use different PNG file types and, although both types can be opened and viewed on both platforms, they appear to their best effect on the platforms on which they were created

- PNG files can contain meta-tags – indexing information that can be read by Web search engines when someone is looking for your website

Obtaining images

Images for insertion in a website can be obtained from a variety of sources:

For an in-depth look at digital photography, have a look at "Digital Photography in easy steps".

- Digital cameras. These are now affordable for the home user and offer a versatile option for creating your own images for a Web page. Digital cameras are now widely accepted in the consumer market and this is an area that is set to increase considerably in years to come. The main advantages of capturing images with digital cameras, as opposed to traditional film cameras and then scanning the images, is that digital cameras do not use any film and images can be viewed as soon as they have been captured. Instead of film, digital cameras use a memory card to store the images. These can then be downloaded to a computer and then removed from the memory card. The memory card can then be used like new. When an image is captured with a digital camera, it is displayed on a LCD panel. This means that you can quickly decide whether you want to keep a particular image or not. If not, you can capture a new one. In addition, when it comes to publishing digital images, you can choose exactly which ones to use, rather than having 36 images processed without knowing what the final quality will be like. This cuts down on the number of wasted images. For anyone who is considering capturing a lot of images for a website a digital camera is an excellent option

With any digital images, regardless of how they are obtained, it is worthwhile using an image editing program to manipulate them once they have been captured.

- Scanners. These can be used to capture existing images in a digital format. Most scanners are similar in design to a photocopier: you place the hard copy on a glass panel and the scanner then moves along the image to capture it. There are various settings that can be used when scanning images and it is important to carefully read the documentation that comes with a specific scanner

As far as capturing digital images is concerned, scanners can be thought of as a flatbed version of a digital camera. The main difference is that you have to bring the image to the scanner instead of taking the camera to the image.

- System clip art collections (most computers come with some items of clip art already pre-installed)

- CD-ROMs. There are several CD-ROMs on the market that contain tens of thousands of graphical and photographic images

Image size

If possible, try and keep images for the Web under 100K in size.

When capturing images with a scanner it is possible to set both the resolution and the desired output size. For images that are going to be displayed on the Web, set the resolution to 72 ppi and then enter the size you want the image displayed at. Since the monitor displays at approximately 72 ppi, the output size you enter should be roughly the size that the image is displayed on the screen.

A lot of digital cameras on the market today are capable of capturing images at sizes that are far too big for publication on a Web page. If you are going to be using a digital camera just for Web images then an entry-level one would be more than adequate for your needs.

One of the most important factors when using images on websites is the overall file size of the images. This is because the file size determines how quickly an image will be downloaded onto a Web page: the bigger the file size, the longer it will take to download. Since this determines how long the user has to wait until the page they have requested appears the importance of image size cannot be underestimated. As Web users become more sophisticated they also become more impatient and do not expect to wait more than a few seconds for a page to appear.

Images on a monitor

One way to ensure a reasonably small file size is to capture the original image at as small a size as possible. With a digital camera this means that you can usually capture images at the lowest settings (i.e. minimum resolution and maximum compression) that your camera will allow. This will probably be in the range of 640 pixels by 480 pixels. The reason for this is that most computer monitors display 72–96 pixels per inch (ppi). Therefore an image captured at 640 x 480 will be displayed on a monitor at approximately 8 x 6 inches (640/72 and 480/72). For a Web page this is still a large image, as far as the physical size is concerned (probably too large in most cases). Anything captured at a higher resolution would create an image that was too large to be displayed easily on a Web page and would have to be reduced in size to make it usable. In the case of Web images, bigger is not always better and in a lot of cases the opposite is true.

Optimizing images

Some image editing programs, such as Macromedia Fireworks and Adobe Photoshop, contain functions for optimizing images. This is a technique where some of the redundant color information is discarded in order to reduce the file size. There are a variety of settings that can be altered to help reduce the size and each of them can be previewed so that the overall effect can be viewed on the image. This is an excellent technique for Web images as it produces good quality images at very small file sizes. If you are going to be using a lot of images on a website, or creating a corporate website, then it would be worth considering a program that can optimize your images. The users of the pages will certainly thank you and it could result in more people visiting a site.

Editing images

In addition to optimization, there are a number of ways to edit images to alter the way they are displayed on the Web.

Editing with the HTML

Changing the size at which an image is displayed does not change the physical file size of the image. This should be done in an image editing program.

As shown in Chapter Three it is possible to alter the physical size at which an image is displayed on a page. This uses the following piece of HTML code:

```
<p><img src="Nick Vandome3.jpg">
width="300" height="330">
```

This code just alters the output display of the image, it does not change the physical file size of the image. Therefore, in terms of image size, it does not really improve the page as far as downloading time is concerned. In this respect it is much better to use a proper image editing program to edit images before they are inserted into Web pages.

Image editing programs

If you are using a lot of images on Web pages you will find it very frustrating unless you are using an image editing program.

There is an enormous range of image editing programs on the market. These range from the professional programs such as Photoshop and Paint Shop Pro, to the entry level programs such as Photoshop Elements and Ulead Express. There are also a large number of shareware programs that can be downloaded from the Web and most of them can be found on CNET at www.cnet.com

Image editing programs allow you to perform numerous tasks including:

Editing digital images can be a very satisfying experience and once you start doing it you may find that all of the images you use become digitally enhanced in one way or another.

- Resizing images

- Basic color management such as adjusting the brightness and contrast

- Removing blemishes and red-eye

- Duplicating items

- Removing unwanted elements

Editing image size

Most image editing programs, whether they are professional or entry level, provide a function for reducing the physical dimensions of an image, and therefore the overall file size. This is done in an image size dialog box, which in most programs can be accessed from the standard menu bar. Once this has been done the image can then be entered into a HTML page and you do not have to worry about resizing it any more.

The larger the number of pixels in an image then the greater the overall file size.

Before resizing:

Adobe are the market leader in image editing software and have a number of products, for all levels of users. For more information on Photoshop Elements have a look at "Photoshop Elements in easy steps". For more information on Photoshop have a look at "Photoshop CS in easy steps".

The original size, as pixel dimensions, is displayed here. (This is from Photoshop Elements, Adobe's entry-level image editing program)

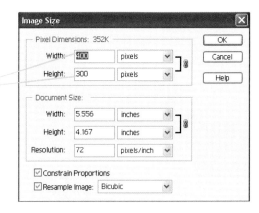

After resizing:

Whatever the pixel dimensions of an image, divide the height and width figures by 72 to work out the approximate size (in inches) at which the image will be displayed on a Web page. For example an image that is 72 pixels by 72 pixels will be displayed on a Web page at approximately 1 inch by 1 inch.

If new dimensions are entered for the physical size of the image then the overall file size is altered (in this example, it decreases from 352K to 88K)

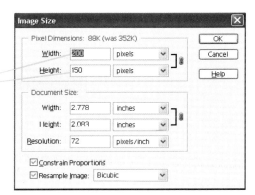

Cropping

Another way to reduce the overall size of an image file is to crop it i.e. remove part of the image altogether. This is not only an effective way to reduce the file size, it is also an important technique for improving images by removing unwanted background elements and concentrating on the central subject. The process for cropping images is similar in most image editing programs:

Always create a copy of an image before you start any image editing. Therefore, if it all goes wrong you still have the copy of the original to fall back on.

Very few images are captured perfectly first time and most would benefit from some cropping before they are used on a Web page.

Most image-editing programs have an Undo command which undoes any editing that has been undertaken. In some programs this is just the most recent command that has been applied while in other programs numerous previous actions can be undone.

1 Using the Crop tool, click and drag to select the area of the image that is to be retained

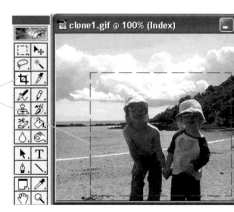

2 Select the Image>Crop command

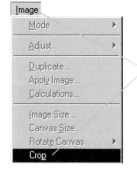

3 The unwanted part of the image is removed, improving the overall composition and reducing the file size

Thumbnails

Make sure that any thumbnails are large enough so that it is clear as to what is being depicted in the image.

Using thumbnail images is an excellent way to include images within a website at a very small size, both physically and in terms of file size. A thumbnail image is a miniaturized version of a larger image. It can be displayed on a Web page, with an accompanying note to say that the larger version of the image can be viewed by clicking on the thumbnail. This way, the user can see what the image contains and they can then choose to view the larger version or ignore it if it is not relevant. Thumbnails are a good way to display numerous images on a single page with each one linking to the larger version:

- **Particularly useful if there are a lot of images on a page**

When creating a thumbnail, make a copy of the original image and then resize this in an image editing program so that it appears on screen at approximately 1 inch square. (This equates to roughly 72 pixels square.) Insert this into a Web page and create another page containing the image at its original size. Then add a hyperlink to the thumbnail that links to the page containing the larger version of the image.

Click on the image to see it at full size

Click on a thumbnail image to view the larger version. This is achieved by adding a hyperlink to the thumbnail image. This can link to a new page which contains the larger version

Thumbnails enlarged

Images and text

Adding text to images is an effective way to give them an individual touch and help them stand out on a page. It is also a useful device for adding additional information to an image. Most image editing programs contain a text tool that can be used to add text to an image (this example is from Photoshop Elements):

Select an appropriate text tool. Some programs allow for horizontal and vertical text to be added

Most image editing programs use a proprietary file format for saving images, in addition to the standard Web formats such as JPEG, GIF and PNG. When adding text to an image it is a good idea to save a copy of the finished version in the proprietary format as well as the format required for use on the Web.

This is because once the image has been exported into a Web format you will no longer be able to edit the text independently, it just becomes part of the whole image. But if it is saved in a proprietary format, this offers more flexibility for editing. It can be opened again, editing changes can be made to the text and then the image can be exported again into a Web format.

2 Select formatting options such as font, size alignment and color

3 Add text by clicking on the image and typing. The text appears in a text box on a separate layer on the image. The text can be edited by double-clicking on the text box

Rollover images

Rollovers work by instructing the Web browser in which the page is being displayed to swap the currently displayed image with a second one, when the cursor passes over the initial image. Then, when the cursor rolls away from the image, the original one is replaced.

Rollover effects have become increasingly common on Web pages in recent years, despite the fact that they are very complex to create from scratch as they are produced with Javascript. However, with a professional Web authoring program it is now possible to produce rollovers quickly and without any knowledge of Javascript.

A rollover image is one that changes appearance when the cursor is passed over it. It can be created with photographic images or graphics such as Web buttons that can be used in page navigation. The following example shows how to create a rollover image using Macromedia Dreamweaver, which is one of the most popular and effective professional Web authoring programs on the market:

1 Create the two images that you want to use for the rollover. Make sure they have the same dimensions because they will be produced at the same size in the rollover

When creating rollover images, make sure that both of the images are the same size, otherwise the second image will be distorted to fit the same space as the first image.

2 Insert the cursor where you want the rollover to appear

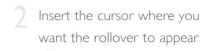

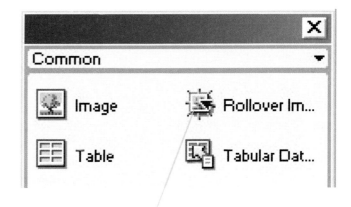

3 Click the Rollover Image button on the Common pane of the Objects palette

One effective device is to use the same image for both the initial image and the rollover one. However, edit the rollover image to have a different color, or some degree of transparency. This will then produce a subtle effect when the rollover is activated.

4 Click here to enter a name for the rollover button

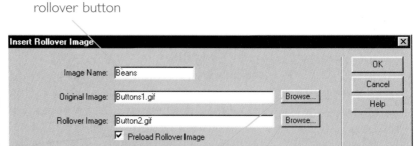

URL stands for Uniform Resource Locator and it is a unique address for every page on the Web. It is usually in a format similar to "www.mysite.com"

If you are linking to a page on your own site, you only need to insert the page name i.e. "news.htm". But if you want to link to an external website, you will need to insert the full URL, which can be copied from the address bar in the browser when you are viewing the page.

5 Click here to locate the first image you are going to use. Repeat the process by clicking here for the second image

6 If you want the user to be able to go to another Web page when they click, click here to select a page to link to. Click OK to create the rollover

Testing the rollover

1 To test a rollover in Dreamweaver, save the file and press F12

2 Or select File>Preview in Browser from the menu bar

Multimedia

Websites have developed considerably since the days of plain text and, if you were lucky, static images. Today's Web designers have an array of devices available to liven up every type of website. This chapter looks at some of the multimedia effects that can be used on Web pages and how to get the best out of them, without overdoing it.

Covers

Chapter Ten

Sound

Digital sound files can be added to Web pages to give them an extra dimension in terms of content. However, a few points should be kept in mind when using sound on a Web page:

Despite the high-profile problems that the online music-sharing website, Napster, has had in relation to making copyrighted music widely available over the Web, there are still a large number of sites that offer similar music. However, the use of this type of material should be avoided if possible, particularly on websites where it is more high profile than if it were on your own computer.

- Users have to have a sound card installed on their computer in order to be able to hear an audio file that has been inserted in a page. This should not be a problem for the majority of users but it could be an issue if you are designing pages for an internal corporate network i.e. an intranet

- Even the most subtle sound effect can become annoying if it plays continuously. With most sound files it is possible to specify the number of times it plays on the page, or the user can decide when they want to activate it

- Do not use copyrighted material on Web pages. Although this is easy to do, sometimes inadvertently, it is nevertheless illegal and should be avoided

Types of sound files

There are a number of different formats for sound files that can be used on the Web, each of which has slightly different properties:

If an audio file format requires a plug-in in order for it to play you will be alerted to this fact when you try and access the file. When pages are being created it is helpful to put a note on the page alerting users to the fact that they require a particular plug-in in order to be able to hear the sound file.

- .MIDI or .MID (Musical Instrument Digital Interface) Provides good sound quality and relatively small file size. This format is supported by most browsers, which can play it without the need for a plug-in (a program that provides the functionality to display or play certain file formats)

- .WAV (Waveform Extension) Provides good sound quality but larger file size than the MIDI format. This format is supported by most browsers, which can play it without the need for a plug-in

- .AIF (Audio Interchange File Format, or AIFF) Similar to WAV in terms of sound quality and file size

- .MP3 (Motion Picture Experts Group Audio, or MPEG-Audio Layer-3) A compressed audio format that provides excellent quality. To play MP3 files, visitors must download and install a helper application, or plug-in, such as QuickTime, Windows Media Player or RealPlayer. This has become one of the most popular and widely used audio formats on the Web

The QuickTime plug-in can be downloaded from the Apple website at www.apple.com; the Windows Media Player can be downloaded from the Microsoft website at www.microsoft.com; and the RealPlayer can be downloaded from the Real website at www.real.com

- .RA, .RAM, .RPM, or Real Audio. A format that uses a high degree of compression to produce relatively small file sizes, although the quality is slightly inferior to MP3. Users require the RealPlayer plug-in in order to play these types of files

Linking to sound files

There are two ways to insert audio files into a Web page. The first is to create the file, or download it from a non-copyrighted source on the Web, and then add a link to it from a page as you would with any other type of linked item. When inserting a sound file in this way, it is a good idea to include a brief explanation so that the user knows what to expect when they click on the link.

The HTML code for a linked sound file is similar to that for any other type of link, except that the linked file is an audio one:

It is possible to create your own sound files, using a microphone connected to your computer and the basic sound recording software that comes bundled with most computers.

```
<a href="http://www.bbc.co.uk/worldservice/news/
summary.ram">BBC World Service radio</a>
```

When displayed on a Web page there should be some hint for the user that they are accessing an audio file

Embedding sound files

The second way to include audio files on a Web page is to embed them on the page. This means that they will start playing as soon as the user accesses the page, as long as they have the required plug-in to play the file. This is if you want to have background music for any pages on your site. When a file is embedded in a Web page a Player is also inserted to enable the user to have some control over the sound file that is playing. It is possible to change the size at which this Player is displayed. The appearance of the Player will vary depending on the type of plug-in, if any, that is required to play the file. The HTML code used to create an embedded sound file looks like this:

There are numerous websites where general sounds and effects can be downloaded. Some to try include:

- www.mp3.com/
- www.soundamerica.com/
- www.dailywav.com/

```
<body>

<embed src=
"background.aif"
width="288"
width="120">

</embed>

</body>
```

The "width" and "height" parameters can be set to determine the size at which the controls are displayed in the browser

When viewed in a browser, this will be displayed like this:

For people using the Netscape Navigator browser to access embedded sound files, there can be some issues surrounding the types of plug-ins that are required. If you are in doubt, open the file with Navigator to make sure that the required controls are visible.

The relevant plugin for playing the sound is displayed. This can be used to control its operation. By default it will play when the file is accessed.

Video

Unless you have a compelling reason to use it, video is probably best avoided on Web pages. This is simply because of the downloading time – most users will get fed up even before the video has finished downloading. In time, as more people start using broadband connections, the use of video may become more widespread, but that point is at least a year or two away.

It is possible to use video on a website but the most important drawback to this is file size: even a short video clip of a moderate quality creates files that are too large for most websites, particularly if the pages are being downloaded over a 56K, or less, modem. There are three ways to get your own video onto a website:

Analog video

Video created on analogue video cameras can be downloaded onto a computer through the use of a analog-to-video capture card that converts the analog signal into a digital one. However, this can be a slightly complex process and the picture quality deteriorates during the conversion process.

Digital video

Digital video cameras have now fallen in price to a level where they are affordable for users. This makes it easier to download onto a computer (although a capture card known as an IEEE 1394 is still required – this is also known as a FireWire connection which allows for very fast downloading of digital data) and the picture quality is very good.

The Windows XP operating system provides software for editing video once it has been downloaded and there are also a number of commercial products such as Adobe Premiere and Final Cut Pro for the Mac.

Webcams

A third option for creating video on the Web is through the use of a Webcam. This is a small camera that is connected to a computer and it can capture still or video images. They are relatively cheap (usually under $100) and they all come with their own software that make the process of making videos relatively painless.

The quality of video captured with a Webcam is usually inferior to that captured with a video camera. Due to their limited resolution the final video can only really be displayed at a small size.

Webcams are cheap and can produce video and still images. However, the quality is limited and the file size is still too large for most Web pages

Animation

Static images are a useful addition to websites but animated images can, if used carefully, add an extra dimension to the graphical content of a website. However, these types of images should be used sparingly — if there are too many spinning, flashing or moving images on a page then the user may either be detracted from the rest of the content on the page or they may be put off altogether. Animated images can either be downloaded from sites on the Web or they can be created manually using a program such as Flash.

Try to limit the use of animated GIFs to one or two per page. Otherwise it may look too "busy" i.e. too much happening on the page. Also, don't use animated images as recurring features on numerous pages. This is much more effective with static images.

Downloading animations

There are thousands of animated images that can be downloaded from sites on the Web. These are almost exclusively in the format of animated GIFs. These are usually fairly small animations that take up relatively little file space. Once the animations have been downloaded they can then be inserted into a Web page in the same way as a static image. Some websites to look at for downloading animated GIFs include:

- www.animfactory.com/

- www.animatedgif.net/

- www.webdeveloper.com/animations/

Sites containing animated GIFs usually provide a simple process for downloading images from the site

Most animated GIFs can be downloaded for free from their respective websites. However, make sure that there are no copyright notices or restrictions on use. Some sites will require you to register before you are able to download images, but this is usually a reasonably straightforward process.

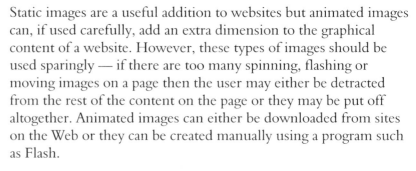

Instructions:
1. PC users should right click on the image of choice
2. Then select "Save image as..."
3. Save image to your harddrive in a folder

Or... **Click Once on an image** to view it alone (faster!!)

Flash

Flash is a professional animation program from Macromedia that can be used to create long animated sequences or small animations similar to animated GIFs. Animations can be created and then saved in a variety of formats, including SWF, GIF and EXE. The finished article is usually known as a Flash movie and there are a number of uses to which these can be put:

- Introductory sequences to websites

- Instructional devices to demonstrate complex processes

- Online displays to show how to perform a certain process such as filling in a complicated form

- Creating small animated effects such as animated logos

If you use Flash to create an opening sequence for a website, make sure that there is a plain HTML alternative and include a link to allow the user to skip the Intro if so desired. (This is particularly important for when users return to the site after their initial visit.)

Skip Intro button

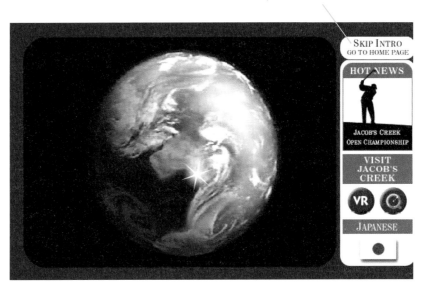

The Flash environment

There is a fairly steep learning curve when using a program such as Flash. Its operating environment is based on the process of creating separate content on different frames within the software. When the frames are played consecutively the whole animation is then displayed. This is similar to drawing different images on the corners of pages of a notebook and then creating the animated effect by flicking through the pages.

In addition to standard animations, Flash can also be used to perform complex functions through the use of its proprietary ActionScript programming language, which is similar to Javascript.

A 30-day trial of Flash can be downloaded from the Macromedia website at www. macromedia.com/

In order to be able to view Flash movies, the user has to have the Flash Player plug-in installed. This is pre-installed in some browsers, but if you do not have it, it can be downloaded from the Macromedia website as above.

Content is placed in the authoring environment. This then occupies a single frame on the timeline

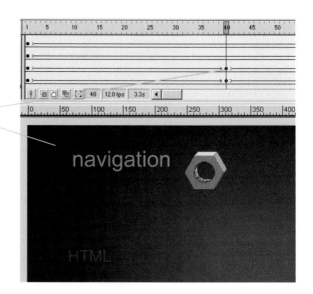

Move to another frame and enter different content. When the frames are played, each frame's content will be displayed in turn.

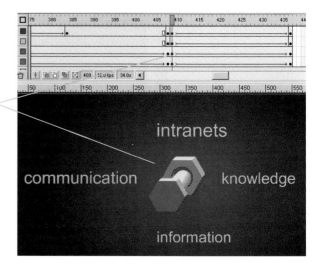

Javascript and DHTML

Javascript and DHTML (Dynamic HyperText Markup Language) are two forms of computer programming language that can be used to add functionality to websites. This includes items such as clocks, news tickers, scrolling text and pop-up menus. To create these from scratch requires a certain amount of computer programming knowledge but, luckily, there are websites where the code can be downloaded and then inserted into an existing HTML page. These sites even have instructions as to where the code is to be inserted within the HTML code. Some sites to try for downloading Javascript and DHTML effects are:

A lot of Javascripts create unusual effects with text. This can look quite dramatic at first but people can tire of them quite quickly.

- http://javascript.internet.com

- www.sitenavigation.net/dhtmlmenu.html

- http://software.xfx.net/mainindex.htm

Javascript sites

Sites that contain Javascripts for downloading usually list the available scripts and their functions and then offer details about how to download and incorporate them into HTML pages:

Compared to HTML, Javascript is a very unforgiving language. If you get one comma or full stop in the wrong place then the code will probably not run and the browser will display a warning dialog box that says there is an error in the syntax of the script.

Once Javascript has been added to a Web page, it has to be viewed in a browser to see the effect.

The JavaScript Source: Clocks: Alarm Clock

Simply click inside the window below, use your cursor to highlight the script, and copy (type Control-c or Apple-c) the script into a new file in your text editor (such as Note Pad or Simple Text) and save (Control-s or Command-s). The script is yours!!!

[Highlight All]   Script Size: 5.28 KB

```
<!-- THREE STEPS TO INSTALL ALARM CLOCK:

  1.  Copy the coding into the HEAD of your HTML document
  2.  Add the onLoad event handler into the BODY tag
  3.  Put the last coding into the BODY of your HTML document  -->

<!-- STEP ONE: Paste this code into the HEAD of your HTML document  -->

<HEAD>

<SCRIPT LANGUAGE="JavaScript">
<!-- Original:  John Caranta (caranta@netzero.net) -->

<!-- This script and many more are available free online at -->
<!-- The JavaScript Source!! http://javascript.internet.com -->

<!-- Begin
var alarmTime;
var curTime;
```

Did you use this script? Do you like this site? Please link to us!

DHTML sites

Sites that offer DHTML effects allow users to download the code required to create these effects or, in some cases, you can download specific programs that enable you to create DHTML items such as pop-up menus:

Pop-up menus can be used to create very stylish navigation systems. These are menus that expand to additional levels when the cursor is rolled over them. If you are creating these types of menu, try and keep the colors and text reasonably subtle – the effect itself should be enough to catch the users' attention.

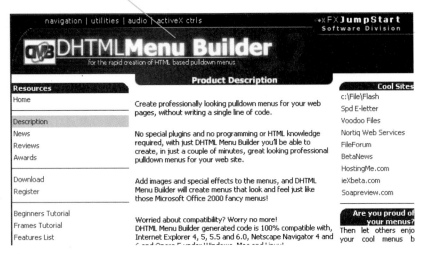

With DHTML designed menus, when you rollover one item, a submenu appears. This structure can be created for as many submenus as are required

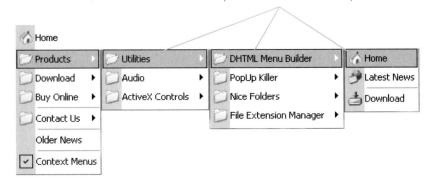

Publishing

The final part in the Web page creation process is getting a site published on the World Wide Web so that everyone can see it. This chapter looks at the process of publishing Web pages and shows how to prepare a site for publication and then keep it well maintained once it has been let loose on the Web.

Covers

Chapter Eleven

Testing

Once the pages of a website have been created they should be put through a rigorous testing procedure before they are published. If there are any errors on your pages, the users will definitely notice them and this could have a detrimental effect on the usage of your site. Some areas to look at for testing include:

Uploading is a term that refers to the process of copying files from your own computer onto the computer (server) that is going to be hosting your site on the Web.

One other type of browser that is gaining popularity on the Web is called Opera. It is a compact and efficient browser that downloads pages more quickly than both of its larger rivals. For more information, have a look at the Opera website at www.opera.com/

If you do not have another monitor to check your site on, contact some computer-owning friends to see if they would be willing to check your site on their machines. This will enable you to see how it appears on a different system and it always helps to get a second opinion about a site.

- Check spelling and grammar. Online publications should be checked as thoroughly as you would with a hard copy publication. Just because it is being viewed on the Web is no excuse for allowing sloppy spelling or grammar. A mistake is a mistake, whether it is in hard copy or online

- Check all links. Make sure that all hyperlinks go to their intended location and that the pages open up as expected. Do this again once the site has been loaded onto the Web, to make sure that all of the relevant files have been uploaded

- Check ALT tags. Make sure all of your images are labelled with ALT tags, particularly for disabled users who are using access technology to read your Web pages. Also, it is seen as good practice in Web design

- Check in different browsers. Even if your site appears perfect when viewed through your own browser this does mean that it will look like this on all browsers. Each browser displays pages slightly differently, particularly items such as Javascript, frames and even tables. Check your pages in a minimum of two browsers, preferably the two most widely used, Internet Explorer and Netscape Navigator

- Check on a large and small monitor. Depending on how your pages have been designed they may appear differently on different sized monitors. This is particularly true if you have used tables set to a specific pixel size – on some monitors this may be completely visible but on a smaller one, some of the content may be obscured

- Check file size. The larger the file size the longer pages take to download. Check the size of any images and if they seem too large either use another image or reduce the size

Transferring to the Web

Once all of the pre-publication checks have been completed you can then think about preparing to publish your pages onto the Web. This is usually done by copying all of the files that are contained within your site (HTML files, image files and multimedia files) from your computer onto the computer that is going to host your site on the Web. This is known as the server. If you have an Internet connection then the company that provides this (your Internet Service Provider or ISP) will almost certainly have a facility for hosting your Web pages. Check in the online help to find out details about how to publish a site and the information that your ISP requires.

If you do not upload all of the files that are within your website structure then there may be gaps on your pages, where images should be, or links will be broken and not work.

Most ISPs have a Web hosting service and there will be details on their site about how to use it

If your website is being hosted by your ISP, your Web address (URL) will be a combination of the company's name and your own sign in name. If you want to have a unique URL – e.g. www. nickvandome.com – then you will have to register a domain name. There are several companies on the Web that offer this service and there is usually a fee, although these can vary considerably. See page 183 for details.

Your ISP will probably offer a range of services for Web hosting. Select the one that is most appropriate for your needs

Web Hosting Package	StarterSite		ProSite		PremiumSite	
Operating system	UNIX	Windows 2000	UNIX	Windows 2000	UNIX	Windows 2000
Monthly fee	$19.95	$24.95	$34.95	$39.95	$84.95	$89.95
Setup fee	$25	$25	$25	$25	$25	$25
Disk space	200MB	200MB	300MB	300MB	500MB	500MB
Data transfer	10GB per month	10GB per month	20GB per month	20GB per month	30GB per month	30GB per month
Mailboxes	30	30	100	100	200	200
	Select This	Select This	Select This	Select This	Select This	Select This
	Tell me about other features, including additional e-mail boxes and disk space					

The process for transferring files onto the Web is known as FTP which stands for File Transfer Protocol. This is a relatively straightforward concept: a program copies the files on your computer and then places them on the destination server. This in effect creates a mirror of the files on your own computer, which ensures that the site will operate in the same way.

FTP can also be used to copy files from other computers onto your own and it is a common way to distribute files between computers on the Web.

1 Using FTP to transfer files from your computer onto your Web hosting server is similar to copying files from one folder to another on your own hard drive

When working with an FTP program the location where the files are kept on your computer is known as the local site and the equivalent one on the hosting server is known as the remote site.

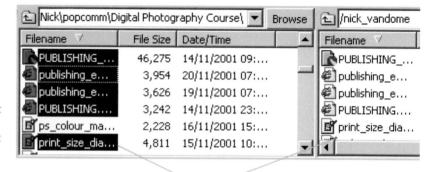

2 There are two panels, one which represents your computer and one which represents the hosting server. When the files have been transferred the two panels should contain the same files

Uploading files to a remote Web server with an FTP program requires an active Internet connection.

FTP programs

Some professional programs, and also HTML editors, have FTP capabilities built in to them. However, if you do not have this facility, a separate FTP program can be downloaded from the Web. Some sites that provide FTP programs are:

- WS_FTP at www.ipswitch.com

- BulletProofFTP at www.bpftp.com

- Fetch at http://fetchsoftworks.com (for Mac users)

These can be obtained by logging on to one of the sites and clicking on the Download button (the following procedure is for BulletProofFTP):

Although most FTP programs list an impressive sounding array of functions, their main task in life is to copy files from one location to another. One useful feature to look out for though is Auto-Reconnect. This means that if your Internet connection is broken while you are uploading files the FTP program will automatically reconnect to the Internet and resume the upload from the point at which the connection was broken.

1 Click on the download button

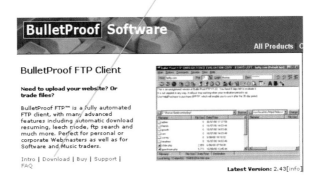

There are a lot of websites that offer excellent FTP programs for free, so if you are asked for payment on any site, move on to another. Some programs are provided free in the Lite version, while the Professional version has to be paid for.

2 Read the downloading instructions and click here to copy the FTP installation program onto your computer

Try BPFTP Client for FREE Now!

You can try a fully functional version FREE for 30 days, it takes just minutes to download and setup. You'll have access to free e-mail support and our online and in-program help should you need it, but BulletProof also means user friendly!

Requirements:

- Windows 95/98/NT/2000/ME/XP/2003
- An internet connection - any speed.
- Less than 1 megabyte of hard disk space, and very little memory, BPFTP is **not** bloatware.

Click here for free download. (3.0 Meg.)

Using FTP

Once you have obtained an FTP program, it can then be used to move files from your own computer onto the server that is hosting your website. This can be either a dedicated Web hosting company, your own ISP or an online Web publishing service such as Yahoo GeoCities or Apple HomePage.

1   Enter the required FTP settings for the computer you want to transfer your files to

For a more detailed look at all of the required FTP settings, see page 186. Where required these will be provided to you by the company or online service that is hosting your site.

2   Select the local files that you want to transfer

The company hosting your website, whether it is your ISP, an online publishing site or a dedicated Web hosting service, will be able to provide you with all of the information that you will require for the FTP settings.

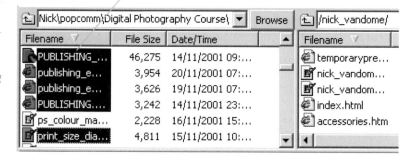

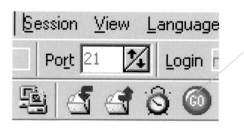

3   Click on the Go button to transfer the files. In some FTP programs this will be a Put button or a directional arrow

Search engines

"Search engine" is a general term used for websites that offer a facility for searching the Web for specific items. There are two main types of search engines: crawler-based services and human-based directories. Both of these catalogue websites in different ways and it is valuable to understand how they both work. Both types of search engines create catalogues of information about websites, which can then be searched by users by entering keywords or phrases into a search field on the search site.

All search engines catalog information slightly differently but usually it is a combination of meta tag information, information displayed on the home page, relevance of page content and meta tags, page title and links from other sites to your own.

Crawler-based search engines

A crawler-based search engine catalogues information by using a small program that automatically searches through a website and catalogues all of the information on a page and also any links that go from the page. These programs are known as crawlers, spiders or bots. Once all of this information has been captured by the crawler it is placed in an index that can then be searched by the site's search software. Crawler-based search engines usually return to sites every couple of months and catalogue any changes that have been made. Examples of crawler-based search engines include:

*   Google at www.google.com

*   HotBot at www.hotbot.com

Every website owner should strive to get registered with as many search engines as possible. This simply means that the search engine knows of a site's existence.

Human-based directories

Human-based directories rely on the human factor rather than automated programs. The most well-known example of this is Yahoo, where the items in their search directory are indexed by individuals who personally go through websites and catalogue the pages accordingly. This can result in information about sites being included in a searchable database and they can also be included in the listings area within Yahoo:

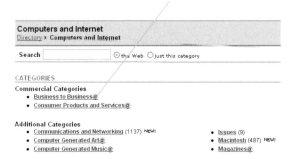

Registering with search engines

There are a number of tricks, such as trying to hide single or multiple words, that Web designers use to try and get a higher ranking with crawler-based search engines. However, the search engines are aware of a lot of these and using such ploys could result in a site being barred from a search engines index.

Crawler-based search engines

Crawler-based search engines can register sites automatically, but first they have to find them. You do this by registering your site with the search engine and then the crawler can go and investigate your site.

Depending on a number of factors, the crawler will index your site and give it a ranking which will be used when people search certain keywords that are related to your site.

To increase your chances of getting a good ranking with a crawler-based search engine it is important to understand how they index information. Some importance is placed on meta tags. These are pieces of code that are placed in the head portion of the HTML document. The two most important meta tags are the description and the keywords tags. The description tag provides the crawler with a brief description of the site content and the keyword tag provides certain words which the search engine can associate with your site. The important thing about description and keyword meta tags is to make sure that they are relevant to the content of your site. One way in which crawlers assess the value of a page is via the meta tags and the page content.

Include plenty of plain HTML links from your home page to all other major areas of your site. This will help a crawler to easily access the rest of your site, which will help the indexing process.

It is also important to include keywords in the content of your page. Imagine the type of words that users will enter in order to search for your site. Then include these words on your home page, either as the page title or as a title or heading on the page itself. The greater the relevance to the content of your pages and the words being used to look for your page, the greater the chance of your page being included in the all important top ten hits.

HTML text is the easiest item for crawler-based search engines to index, rather than a lot of images or Flash movies.

Another important factor when your site is being analyzed by a crawler is how many links come into your site from other related sites. The important word here is related: search engines place a lot of importance on links from sites that contain similar information. So, for instance, if your site is about computer operating systems and you have links from both Microsoft and Apple then a crawler-based search engine would consider this as being very noteworthy and your page would be likely to get a higher ranking as a result.

To submit a site to a crawler-based search engine:

The more relevant information that a crawler can gather from your site, then the better your rating will be when someone searches using a specific keyword.

1 Open the home page of the search engine. Select the options for submitting your site

The more "search-friendly" that your site is then the greater the likelihood that it will receive a higher ranking. This means that when a search is made containing some of the keywords associated with your site, it will appear higher up on the list of results that are returned to the user. This in turn improves the chances of the user then visiting your site.

2 Continue the submission process by selecting the required options and clicking Continue

Once your site has been registered with a search engine, check to see where it appears when searching using different keywords. If necessary, resubmit the site after a few weeks.

Human-based directories

Getting registered with a human-based directory takes a little more effort than just sending your URL to a crawler-based search engine. The following example is for registering with Yahoo, which is far and away the largest human-based directory:

1   Open the Yahoo home page and click on a category that covers the content in your website

Web Site Directory - Sites organized by subject   Suggest your site

Business & Economy
B2B, Finance, Shopping, Jobs...

Regional
Countries, Regions, US States...

Computers & Internet
Internet, WWW, Software, Games...

Society & Culture
People, Environment, Religion...

News & Media
Newspapers, TV, Radio...

Education
College and University, K-12...

Make sure you choose the most suitable category for your site when you are submitting it to a site such as Yahoo. Otherwise it may not even get past the first stage of registration.

2   Drill down through the options until you find a category into which your site fits. Click on the Suggest a Site link

Search [   ] ⊙ the Web ○ just this category   [Search]   Advanced Search | Suggest a Site
                                                                                       email this category to a friend

INSIDE YAHOO!

Internet Access: get **Internet** Access for your home or business from SBC and Yahoo!

SPONSOR RESULTS

Free Comet Cursor
from Comet Systems
Change your mouse pointer
from that boring black and
white arrow into ...
www.cometcursor.com

See your message here...

CATEGORIES

- Billing (30)
- Blocking and Filtering@
- Browsers@
- Chat (47)
- Consumer Software@
- Development (599) NEW!
- Download Managers@
- Electronic Commerce@
- Email@
- Firewalls@

- FTP (45)
- Instant Messaging (36)
- Intelligent Agents (18)
- Internet Telephony@
- Intranet@
- Peer-to-Peer File Sharing@
- Real Time Broadcasting (28)
- Search (63)
- Titles (33)

3 Click here to access the Yahoo! Express service, which requires a fee for listing websites

It is important to read the notes page carefully and follow what it says. Failure to do so could result in your registration being rejected as being unsuitable.

Yahoo! - Help

Suggest a Site to Yahoo!

Yahoo! Express
7-Day Guarantee
US$299.00 non-refundable, recurring annual fee
· Required for commercial listings but available for any site
· Guaranteed and expedited consideration of your site within 7 business days

Learn more...

Submit your site for consideration via
Yahoo! Express

4 Check the required boxes

How to Qualify

To qualify for Yahoo! Express you must meet and accept all of the following conditions.

Please check the box next to each item to indicate that you understand and accept each condition:

☐ I have read and agree to be bound by the **Yahoo! Express Service Agreement.**

☐ I have verified that my site does not appear in the Yahoo! Directory under a different URL and I understand that this is **not** the place to request a change for an existing site. [Section 2.6]

☐ My site supports multiple browsers and capabilities. (For example, Java-only sites will not be listed). [Section 3.1]

☐ My site is in the English language (or has an English language version available). [Section 3.1]

☐ I understand that there is **no guarantee** my site will be added to the Yahoo! Directory. [Section 2.5]

☐ I understand that Yahoo reserves the right to edit my suggestion and category placement; movement or removal of my site will be done at Yahoo!'s sole discretion. [Section 4.1]

☐ I understand that if my site is added, every year thereafter my credit card will be charged the then-current recurring annual fee. [Section 2.4]

☐ My site is up and running 24 hours a day, seven days a week. [Section 3.1]

☐ No part of my site is under construction. All links on the site work. [Section 3.1]

Continue

5 Click Continue

Unless you have a very specialist website, you should be able to find a relevant category for it within the existing listings.

6 Enter details of your site

Welcome, nickvandome   Sign Out
Yahoo! Directory Listings

Yahoo! Express Home > Request New Listing

Request New Listing: Step 2 of 4 - Site and Contact Information

Your Site Information

Enter information about your site below to help us describe and categorize it. Be brief and do not use all capital letters. Yahoo! reserves the right to edit all titles and descriptions.

* Required Fields

Category :   **Not Specified - provide Additional Information below.**

* Site Title: Nick Vandome
· The name of the site. (e.g., Museum of Modern Art)

* URL: www.nickvandome.com
· The web address of the site, beginning with "http://"

7 Enter your contact details

Make sure you enter your contact details correctly as these will be used to inform you of anything relating to your registration application.

Contact Information

In the event that we have questions about the placement of this site and to ensure that listings in Yahoo! unauthorized persons, please provide the following:

* **Contact Name:** Nick Vandome

* **Contact Email:** nickvandome@hotmail.com
Verify that the email address above is correct.

Submit

8 Click Submit

Multiple registrations

If you want you can visit each of the major search engine sites in turn and submit your site for registration to each one. However, it is much quicker to use a site that takes a lot of the online leg work out of the process and sends submissions to all of the major search engine sites. One site that does this is SubmitExpress at www.submitexpress.com. To make multiple submissions using SubmitExpress:

The term multiple registration is used here in connection with submitting a single website to numerous search engines. It does not refer to submitting the same site on several different occasions. This is done by some Web authors, in the hope that it will increase their chances of being ranked more highly by the search engines.

In fact the reverse is probably true. This practice is known as spamming and is frowned upon by search engine sites. In some cases, it may even lead to sites being barred from a search engine.

1 Click here to select the type of submission you want to make

2 Click here to have meta tags for your site generated automatically

FREE WEBSITE SUBMISSION

website URL to 40 top search engines for free.

es, CLICK HERE to make sure you are using th vantage of our free META Tag Generator for bes ltiple submissions of the same URL to some se from being listed.

Sites such as SubmitExpress usually allow you to resubmit your site once a month. This ensures that the search engines have the most up-to-date information about your site and it can help to correct any mistakes that have crept into the Index.

Website Title: (Up to 100 characters)

Description: (2-3 sentences. Do not use RETURNs)

Keywords: (Separated by commas, try to use 2 word phrases as well, up to 255 characters)
Not sure what keywords to use? CLICK HERE

Would you like your page to be indexed by Search Engines?
○ YES ○ NO

Would you like the search engines to follow links on your site for further indexing?
○ YES ○ NO

Author's Email Address:

Generate META Tags   Reset Form

3 Enter the relevant details and click on the Generate META Tags button

4 Return to the submission page and enter the site details here. Click on Submit

URL: http://www.nvandome.com

Your email: nickvandome@hotmail.com

Sign up for FREE newsletters and mailing lists for the latest news

☑ Submit Express Newsletter. Search engine news and promotion tips

☑ Affiliate Express Newsletter. Includes affiliate program reviews and re

☐ Books   ☐ Finance-Investing

☐ Business Opportunities   ☐ Internet-Shoppers

☐ IT Professionals   ☐ Small business owners

☐ Affiliate Programs   ☐ Internet Marketing

☐ Credit Cards   ☐ Web Design and Promotion

Submit

It can take a few moments for the results to appear after you have clicked on the Submit button.

SubmitExpress also have a paid option that submits your website to 75,000 search engines. This is not really necessary: if your site cannot be found using the main 40 search engines then it is probably pretty well hidden.

Thank you for using Submit Express.

Your website at http://www.nvandome.com was submitted to the search engines listed below.

You asked to subscribe to one of our mailing lists. Please note you will be sent a confirmation MUST receive your reply in order to activate your subscription. If we don't receive your reply, w you the mail you have requested! You MUST check your mail and reply. If you like to subscribe click here.

We provide this service for free. All we ask in return is to put the following button and link on yo

Submit *to 40 Top Search Engines*

Free search engine submission and placement services!

5 The confirmation page informs you that your site has been submitted to the listed search engines. Click on this link to see how you can improve your chances of achieving a high placement in search engine results

Marketing a site

If you want to find websites that may include a link to your own site, look carefully at them and check before you approach them. Considerations such as location of the site's author and whether or not they include links to other sites or not are important factors.

In addition to promoting your site by registering it with search engines and trying to get a high listing, it is also a good idea to market your site through other methods too. Only a limited amount of site traffic is generated by search engines (as little as 16% according to some surveys) and so it is important to make as many people as possible aware of your site. The key point with this is to market your site to people who will have a reason to use it. There is little point in undertaking a marketing campaign aimed at yachting enthusiasts if your site is about egg-cup collecting. Some ways to market your site include:

- Ask related websites to include a link to your site on their own one. This will only work if you can include a reciprocal link on your site and the two sites must complement each other – if you approach someone who is a direct competitor they are unlikely to add your link to their site

- Include your website address in any hard copy literature you send out. This could be business cards, magazines, brochures or even personal letters

Do not send emails containing your Web address indiscriminately to individuals or companies. This type of unsolicited approach is known as spamming and is frowned upon by most Internet users.

- Include your website address with any emails you send. This could be included in the signature, which is an element of an email that can be automatically included whenever a message is sent

- Attract some press coverage. Feature pages in newspapers and magazines carry a lot of items about new and interesting websites. Have a look at some of these and approach those that you think may be interested in writing about your site. If it covers an unusual or obscure topic then you may have more of a chance of getting some press coverage

- Take out advertising. High profile advertising campaigns have accounted for large parts of the budget for many of the dotcom companies that have gone bankrupt since 2000. However, you do not have to spend hundreds of thousands of pounds to have a successful advertising campaign. Posters in shops and advertisements in local free newspapers are a good way to attract a local audience to your site

Maintaining a site

Do not fall into the trap of putting a "last updated" date on a website and then not changing it for months, or years. A guaranteed method of ensuring users depart from your website immediately is to have a "last updated" date that is several months previously.

In some ways, the easy part about creating a successful website is the initial creation and publication of the pages. The hard part is then ensuring that it is up to date and well maintained.

Update information

One of the most crucial elements for any website is to reassure users that the site is actually maintained on a regular basis. This can be done with a "Last Updated" date. However, this on its own does not necessarily mean much – if the user does not know when the site is next going to be reviewed this type of information can be irrelevant. A better system is to have a "Last Updated" date, followed by a "Next Review Date Due". This way any visitors can see how frequently the site is reviewed and updated. If there are no changes to be made when the review date arrives this can still become the "Last Updated Date" and a new review date set. As long as the users are confident that the site has been looked at then they will be happy to return at a later date. This system of updating a site should be included somewhere on the home page and, if required, on subsequent site pages too:

The "Last Updated" and "Next Review Date Due" items can be included with the site navigation bar so that it is visible on every page of the site. In some cases, individual pages may have different review dates depending on the type of information that they contain.

<u>Home</u> | <u>IT Books</u> | <u>Training Courses</u> | <u>Travel Books</u> | <u>Tips and Hints</u> | <u>Email me</u>

Last updated 08/24/2004

Next review due 10/20/2004

© Nick Vandome 2004

If you have a very current site, such as a news site, there will be no need for a "Next Review Date Due" item as it will be expected that the site will be updated on a continuous basis.

A robust, and visible, system of site revision is a vital component in ensuring that visitors to your site can be confident that the information is up to date and well maintained.

Domain names

One of the drawbacks of an online Web publishing service hosting your website is that they will not allow you to select your own Web address. In most cases it will be a combination of the company's name and your own username.

This does not always look good if you want to use your site for professional purposes. This is also true for the basic service offered by ISPs to host a site. However, most of them also offer a fee-based service for registering domain names and hosting the subsequent sites. Check your ISP's online documentation for details.

If you decide you want to publish your website without the restrictions of online publishing or being hosted by your ISP, another alternative is to register for a unique Web address, such as www.nickvandome.com. This costs an annual fee and there are several companies that offer this service. Three to look at are:

- Network Solutions at www.netsol.com

- Verisign at www.verisign.com

- Planet Domain at www.planetdomain.com

The process for registering a domain name is as follows:

1. Enter the details of the domain name that you want to register. Click on the Search button

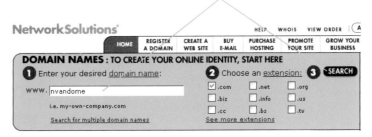

2. You will be informed if your preferred domain name is available

The cost for registering domain names can vary dramatically between companies. Have a look at a minimum of six sites that offer this service before you make a choice.

Once you have registered a domain name, no-one else can register exactly the same name. A domain is the entire URL i.e. http://www.nickvandome.com

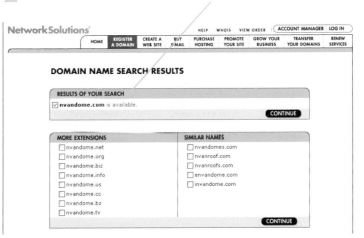

Web hosting

Once you have registered a domain name, you will then need someone to host your site on the Web. Your own ISP should be able to offer this service, but probably only if you have also registered a domain name with them too. Also, ISPs can be more expensive than dedicated Web hosting services. Either way, it pays to shop around before you commit yourself to a Web hosting package.

Web hosting companies usually charge a fee for their services but, as with registering domain names, these vary between companies, so it pays to shop around. There are some Web hosting services which are free, but this is compensated by the fact that advertisements will be included on your site.

In addition to ISPs, there are numerous companies that offer Web hosting and three to look at are:

- Earthlink at www.earthlink.com

- Dream Host at www.dreamhost.com

- Network Solutions at www.networksol.com

The process for registering with a Web hosting service is as follows:

Select the Web hosting option that best suits you

Having your own domain name for your website gives it a more professional appearance, particularly when you are marketing it to other people.

2 Enter your domain name details

NetworkSolutions

HELP   WHOIS   VIEW ORDER   AC

HOME | REGISTER A DOMAIN | CREATE A WEB SITE | BUY E-MAIL | PURCHASE HOSTING | PROMOTE YOUR SITE | GROW YOUR BUSINESS

GET A HOSTING PLAN THAT WORKS FOR YOU

Network Solutions has partnered with ValueWeb to offer you an affordable Standard Web Hosting plan that gives you all of the features you need to build your Web site. In addition to generous disk space and data transfer, you also receive over $150 in free software and services.

1st MONTH FREE AND FREE SET UP

CALL A VALUEWEB EXPERT
1-800-346-1594

▶ STANDARD VALUEWEB HOSTING PLAN FEATURES
- Over $150 of FREE Software
- 200 MB Disk Storage
- 10 GB data transfer
- Virtual secure server
- Virtual FTP server
- 24/7 technical support
- FrontPage 2002 extensions
- Plan Comparison chart

$19.95 a Month

ENTER THE DOMAIN NAME YOU WANT HOSTED WITH VALUEWEB

Enter Domain Name
nvandome.com
(i.e. networksolutions.com)

This is a:
⦿ New domain name
○ Domain registered with Network Solutions
○ Domain name registered with another company

CONTINUE

3 Click Continue

Even when you have registered with a Web hosting service, it may take a few days before you can publish your files onto their server. This is because all of the ISPs have to be informed of the existence of this new site and update their databases so that it can be accessed. This is known as propagation and you should be notified once it has taken place.

4 If you have already registered your domain name, you may have the option of transferring the registration

NetworkSolutions

HELP   WHOIS   VIEW ORDER   ACCOUNT MANAGER

HOME | REGISTER A DOMAIN | CREATE A WEB SITE | BUY E-MAIL | PURCHASE HOSTING | PROMOTE YOUR SITE | GROW YOUR BUSINESS | TRANSFER YOUR DOMAINS

DOMAIN NAME TRANSFER RESULTS

Good news – the domain(s) you want to transfer are eligible for transfer. Check the box next to the domains you would like to transfer and click **Continue**.

- All years you've already purchased will be honored in full by Network Solutions.
- All transfers to Network Solutions include an additional year added to the time remaining on your existing term.
- Risk free – You are only charged when the transfer is successful.
- Add more years to your term for just $19 per year – only available at the time of a transfer to Network Solutions.

For questions about transferring domain names, visit our FAQs.

RESULTS OF YOUR TRANSFER REQUEST

☑ **nickvandome.com** is available to transfer

SEARCH AGAIN   **CONTINUE**

Once you have registered with a Web hosting service you will be sent information, usually by email, about how to publish your site. This will include details about transferring your files with FTP and the settings that you will require. These will include:

- *Host address. This is the address on the host's server where your files will be sent*

- *Remote directory. This is the folder into which your files will be placed*

- *A site label. This can be anything that you want, as it is your record of the site name*

- *User ID. This will usually be the main part of your domain name e.g. nickvandome.com*

- *Password. This will be given to you by your Web host. In some cases you can change it to your own password*

5 Review your Web hosting order

NetworkSolutions® HELP WHOIS VIEW ORDER | ACCOUNT MANAGER | LOG IN

| HOME | REGISTER A DOMAIN | CREATE A WEB SITE | BUY E-MAIL | PURCHASE HOSTING | PROMOTE YOUR SITE | GROW YOUR BUSINESS | TRANSFER YOUR DOMAINS | RENEW SERVICES |

VIEW YOUR ORDER

Save money on many Network Solutions services by extending the term of the product you are ordering. Click **Recalculate** to verify the term and price before proceeding to purchase.

Years	Yearly Price	Savings
10	$14.99	57%
5	$19.99	42%
3	$24.99	28%
1	$34.99	-

Savings based on total cost if renewed annually.

YOUR ORDER INCLUDES

	Terms	Your Price ($US)	
Domain Transfer: nickvandome.com	1 Year	$19.00 *	◄ REMOVE
Additional Years Special Price With Transfer	2 Years ▾	$38.00 *	◄ REMOVE

Have an invitation code? Enter it Now

* Deferred Charges - By submitting your order, you are authorizing us to charge you for any registrations and/or transfers we undertake on your behalf. You will not be charged for any Registrations, Transfers or other products & services until we receive confirmation of a successful registration and/or authorization for any transfer.

Deferred Charges*	$57.00
Current Charges	**$0.00**
Total	**$57.00**

RECALCULATE PROCEED TO PURCHASE

6 If you are happy with your order, click the Proceed To Purchase button to process your order and activate your Web hosting service

If you have any problems or queries about the FTP settings, there should be a helpline telephone number or email address to contact.

Index